I AM ESKIMO

Aknik My Name

By Paul Green aided by Abbe Abbott   Illustrated by George Aden Ahgupuk

ALASKA
NORTHWEST
BOOKS®

Library of Congress Cataloging-in-Publication Data available upon request

International Standard Book Number: 978-0-88240-588-9

Published in 1959
Revised Edition published in 2004

Alaska Northwest Books®
An imprint of Graphic Arts Books
P.O. Box 56118
Portland, OR 97238-6118
(503) 254-5591

www.graphicartsbooks.com

Cover Design: Elizabeth Watson

Ahgupuk

Table of Contents

Our old Eskimo had a better way of kissing their friends or girl friends.

Introduction

IT HAS BEEN our good fortune to be able to frequently travel and live among the Eskimo people, and in doing a foreword for this book, there is great temptation to describe to you the lonely beauty of the Arctic land in which the Eskimo lives.

We would like to be able to tell you in great detail of summers where the green-splotched brown of the flat or rolling tundra meets a cold Arctic sea that is sometimes blue, sometimes brown, sometimes milky white, but always cold and seemingly stretching away to the west and on either hand into an infinite distance.

We would like to tell you of the vastness of the white Arctic winter landscape, where the gray of sky, and the gray of tundra snow, and snow-covered ice fields become as one, without shoreline, without horizon, and seeming without ceiling or floor, and the only thing that gives perspective is the silent creeping of streamers of blowing snow at your feet, moving restlessly and endlessly like a thousand tiny white rivers in a white world.

There is much else we would like to tell you of this strange world where the Eskimo lives and the white man is only an occasional visitor, but for all the descriptive phrases we might employ, we cannot help but admit that Paul Green (Aknik), and George Ahgupuk, can do the job so much better.

You will find that a great deal of the charm in this book lies in the Eskimo's ability to make a few words do for many, just as he economically utilizes the few material essentials available to him in his daily business of living in a seemingly harsh and improvident Arctic world.

When the weather is bad, we grumble and talk about it endlessly, belaboring one another with the unfairness of such a thing, blaming the changing seasons, the too-many automobile exhausts, and the too-many atomic explosions "we" or "they" are effecting.

The Eskimo has a phrase I have often heard, which sounds like "Un-oak-luh-stuk."

It is said simply, without emphasis. It means, literally, "It rains—it blows."

If we could be as simple.

I recall still another Eskimo economy in the use of words which I will pass along in hopes that I can give you some little additional understanding of why I love these people, and envy them.

Johnny is an Eskimo. I knew him when he was a young airplane mechanic for an Alaskan bush pilot friend of mine.

One time, Johnny and his pilot employer were taking off in a beat-up old Travelair from a remote mining camp airfield. Their engine was too cold for the proper number of revolutions. Their wings were carrying too much ice for the good air flow that would permit maximum speed.

They barely got off the ground and the old Travelair staggered back to earth in a pile of stumps at the end of the field. The sound of tearing fabric and smashing metal could be easily heard back at the mine camp, a mile from the airport where the superintendent had recently bid the pilot and Johnny goodby and gone back up the hill to his crew.

When Johnny limped back to the airfield phone and called the camp, the superintendent was understandably frantic with apprehension.

"What happened? What happened?" he shouted into the receiver.

Johnny, without emphasis, in his soft, low Eskimo voice, said, "We—crashed."

Then he hung up.

Aknik would have said no more.

ROBERT A. HENNING
Editor
December 1959

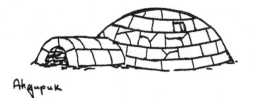

My Mother used to tell me I was born in small snow house.

Ahgupuk

How I Get My Name   1

I AM FULL blooded Eskimo and live in Arctic of Alaska. I was born 1901 January 7 around Kotzebue, Alaska. My mother use to tell me I was born in small snow house. (In early days ago before white man come to Alaska, in winter time, Eskimo woman use to born babies in small snow house, no help, nobody around, all by themself).

My father was Kotzebue man, had two brothers older than him and one sister. So he left his two brother and one sister at Kotzebue and left for Kivalina, and he raise us kids at Kivalina. His older brother's Eskimo name was Na-shook and when white missionary arrived at Kotzebue they gave my uncle Na-shook an English name of Lincoln. His younger brother's Eskimo name was She-koup-she-ruk and white missionary name him in English—Norton. My father's Eskimo name Taluk and white man name him Green. So there you are—three brothers with different last name. And I become known at Kivalina as Paul Green—but my Eskimo name is Aknik.

I live in Kivalina 35 years. Kivalina School House was build 1905. That where I start my first school. Mr. and Mrs. Walton was first teacher at Kivalina and my younger sister was born that year. She live in Anchorage now. That where I learn my first A B C, from Mrs. Walton at Kivalina. Our next teacher was Mr. and Mrs. York and I learn more English words from them.

You know we kids in Arctic of Alaska we learn our education in lumber house like your house in states. Our home was built by lumber and driftwood those days and put sod all around it. No snow igloo, but sod igloo.

Every spring went to Point Hope for whaling. Summer come back to Kivalina and went to Kotzebue with skin boat. Kotzebue place where all Eskimo get together in summer, carve ivory and sell furs. Around September went back to Kivalina for stay. Some time went up the river with skin boat and stay up the river part of the winter. About spring came down to Kivalina. Best trout you ever get is at Kivalina. Some of them BIG trout! There is mineral water right in Kivalina river—way up. Kivalina trout stay fat whole year around. They never get poor like in other river. I think that mineral water way up head of Kivalina river keeps Kivalina trout fat. When it cool weather—real freeze—that place

Our home was built of lumber and driftwood those days. Put sod all around. No snow igloo. Sod igloo.

2

In summer Eskimo go to Kotzebue, carve ivory.

near mineral water always open up—you will never go through with dog sled on river. You have to go over land. When it cloudy, always freeze up in that place. But open on edge—boiling up from under. That water look like tea, some weak—some strong.

My last school was at Noatak. I was 16 when I quit school. I got married 1921 at Point Hope Mission. Later I move to my home town Kotzebue. After few years at Kotzebue I move to Nome and stay at Nome. I had my family with me. I don't know where will be our next move.

Everybody takes furs to trading post. Trade with other Eskimo people too with seal oil, oogruk rope and other things.

3

2 True Story About Arctic of Alaska

IN SPRING TIME we went to Point Hope for whaling and stayed at Point Hope during whaling season and as soon ice goes out we went back to Kotzebue by skin boat. In those day whale bone was pretty high. There were old whalers at Point Hope in those days—Jim Allen, Tom George, Mr. Lieb and Coopers, and some of the native go whaling for themself. Around 1905 there used to be lot of people at Point Hope, come from different villages; from Kivalina, Noatak, Kotzebue, Kobuk and Selawik.

There were seven or eight men in one crew and a cook. The owner of the boat used to hire men for his whaling crew during whaling season. When they start whaling, they went out around 10 or 12 of April, (depend when whale come through). Then they went out with skin boat when it was open water.

They watch for whale night and day—change shift—half the crew sleep and half stayed wake and watching for whale to come up. They never change clothes as long as they stay in open water, but they change their mukluk when they get wet. They never went to sleep in sleeping bag during open water. When they make camp they pull skin boat up on floating ice. They general went to sleep on top of flat sled. (Bring sled along in oomiak to haul meat over ice.) Turn boat on side, put windbreaker around it, so the wind won't blow into them when they sleep. Use hides or canvas for wind-breaker.

Whaling season generally over around June 9 and all the whalers went to shore for big time. Those Captain of the boats that caught whale put up big feast after the whaling season is over. When they had feast, the

4

Hunters watch night and day for whale.
Some sleep. Always someone watch.

crews of the boat that caught whale, they cut up flipper of the whale about ½ inch thick and the captain of the boat pass it to all the people that come to his feast. And all the people eat muk-tuk (whale skin) and mee-kee-gak. (Mee-kee-gak is name for whale meat and muk-tuk put together in seal poke or barrel for eating. People in the Arctic when they caught big bow head whale, they took meat and muk-tuk [whale skin] and put them together in seal poke or barrel and let stand about week in the house without any cooking or without putting anything in it. And the whale meat and muk-tuk get pickle in seal poke or barrel, and the Mama Eskimo watch the meat and muk-tuk when it will be ready to eat. That what they call mee-kee-gak.)

They had all kind of cooking at that feast. They cook everything out doors. Some of the women make doughnut, some of them cook whale meat. They use whale oil for making doughnut same as you do lard. After they had feast, they had big Eskimo dance and big Na-lee-ka-tuk (mean blanket toss).

After Na-lee-ka-tuk all them people went back to their own village with their skin boat. No motor in those days, they use sail when wind just right. When no wind they towed skin boat with dog. They hitch up

After feast they had big Na-lee-ka-tuk (mean blanket toss).

5

Woman pick berries,
blue berries,
all kind of berries.

Ahgupuk

dog on beach and have long rawhide tied to skin boat. And a person, man or woman stayed with dog and have the dogs follow the beach. When the weather permit they keep going night and days, some of them sleep in skin boat while rest of people keep going with skin boat.

In those early days our old folk never work for somebody. They made living out of hunting. They made living out of hunting wild games, fresh meat all the time—hunting seal and foxes and polar bear in winter. Also fishing in winter, hook tom cod, and fishing through ice on river for trout and salmon and white fish; and in spring they dried up fish and seal meat and put them in seal poke with seal oil for winter.

Also women pick berries, blue berries, all kind of berries. Put them in seal poke with little seal oil and put away for winter. Early days ago Eskimo used seal oil like salt. They also dried Oogruk (Bearded Seal) meat and put away for winter.

And in winter time they always have plenty to eat. They don't have to buy meat—not like us Eskimo to-day. I think some days these Eskimo new generation will forget how to talk Eskimo language—they all be talking English. Also forget Eskimo dances. Now today around Nome up to Barrow, some of these Eskimo boys and girls they could not understand Eskimo language; neither they don't know how to dance Eskimo dances.

6

The woman have small place for cooking in storm shed.

Ahgupuk

About Igloos   3

LOT OF PEOPLE in States think igloo is snow house. But it was not. Also, they think we Eskimo that live in Arctic of Alaska use snow house for our home. We Eskimo that live in the Arctic never use snow house for our home unless we get caught in storm. I live in snow house lot of time when I went out hunting. It's a warm home if you fixed it right. That the only time we Eskimo use snow igloo made out of snow, when we went out hunting or when we figure to stay one place about a week we make snow igloo, because we know it was a warm home.

Our great-grandfather use igloos in winter time or in summer. They dig three or four feet in ground and put frame up; put timber right close together; and then put sod all around it and on top; and put the window on top of igloo and put ventilator. They use oogruk guts or walrus guts for their window. Woman sewed them together and used it for their skylight.

Igloo was made out of sod and timber. It was a warm home for us kids in early days ago. Now today we got timber house and use oil stove night and days. In them igloo in early day ago they just use fire in day time—no fire at night. In early day ago before white man come to Alaska —before Eskimo find out about stove—they took off skylight at evening on top sod igloo, and they have big rock around fire place in middle

7

Ahgupuk

Igloo was made out of sod and timber. It was warm place for us kids in early days ago.

of floor, and they build fire and heat them rock. When the rock get red hot they turn out fire and put skylight back on, and the inside of the igloo was pretty warm, just like they have stove going. And the woman have a small place for cooking in storm shed.

4   How to Make Snow Igloo

SAY FRIEND, it a good thing to learn little every thing about make living in Alaska. I was raise by my father Taluk and my mother Mukuk and father taught me in young age how to make sled—Kayak—skin boat—and how to make snow igloo. But my father died in my young age—my father died when I was twelve year old. But I remember what he taught me.

One time a fellow and I went out for trapping, with sled, some deer. I just took sled cover, Swedish stove and grub, shovel and hand saw and my sleeping bag made out of reindeer skin. So other fellow had

Ahgupuk

We take the harness off our sled deer and tied them to clumps of tundra grass.

about same thing I got. But he didn't take no shovel or hand saw and we travel quite a long way that day and kind of getting late so we stop in the river and take the harness off our sled deer and take them up where lot of moss is and tied them to clumps of tundra grass.

When we came back to our sled that other fellow haven't got much to say. It look to me he kind of worry.

I said to him, "What wrong, my friend, what make you worry? No use to worry. Worry, won't help you."

He said, "What make me worry? What we going to have for our tent? Our sled cover too small to make a tent with and it getting late. If we start for home we not going to sleep out door in cold weather like this —that what make me worry."

I said to him, "Did your old folks ever tell you or showed you how to make some kind of home if you get caught in storm?"

He said, "No, they never show me anything."

Now you see, my friend, some of them Eskimo never been living in snow igloo in Arctic of Alaska. If they all been living in snow igloo like you read in books—what them book writers write that came from state they all will know how to make snow igloo. But some of these boys never been told by their old folks how to make snow igloos. That proof we Eskimo in Arctic of Alaska never use snow igloo to raise our family. I told other fellow with me "I'll show you how to make home sweet home, so you will never worry again when you hunt or get caught in storms."

We dig about three feet in hard snow and make it round. I told the guy to cut block of snow and bring it to me any size. So he cut block of snow and bring them to me. And I lay them all around the hole we dig. Next layer I put, I have them 2 inches in from the first layer—

9

Ahgupuk

*In Arctic of Alaska
we stand under
our American Flag.*

and keep up building like that till I had one block on top to cover whole thing. And I take big butcher knife and rounded up our snow igloo and put little hall way about 4 feet and use canvas or deer skin for door after you finish your snow igloo. Please, don't forget to put air hole on top of your snow igloo. Otherwise you won't have any air in your home sweet home. After we finish our snow igloo we put willows on the floor so our mukluk won't get wet. After we put willows on the floor we bring in our sleeping bag, grub and our Swedish stove, and we light our coal oil lamp and our stove. Gee! it sure get hot no time inside our new home.

You know, my friends, one time writer fellow come up here from States. He spend two-three days asking questions and write down all the thing I say in answer to his questions—how we live, how we make living, and so on. So I find out myself how them book writers make book out of me! Long time later I read that book, and some true and some not true. That writer fellow don't write what I tell him true; he write what he think people want to hear about Eskimo in Arctic of Alaska and you people in States believe that how we live. I think, if I went out and spend two or three day in States and write a book about people in States, and say lot of things that wasn't true and make my people believe that how people in States live, I know myself nobody in States would like me if I wrote about them what was not true.

I hope some of these days book writer come to Arctic of Alaska and write true story about us Eskimo. We are true citizen of U.S.A. not adoption citizen. In the Arctic of Alaska we stand under our American Flag.

Our old generation use snare for ducks.

About Hunters 5

OUR GREAT grandfathers don't have gun, no kind of gun to hunt with. But they were raise as good hunter. They use bow arrow, spear and spade and knife for hunting, and they use snare and sling for duck. They also use snare for deer, rabbit and ptarmigan.

In early days ago our old generation use bow arrow for deer, bear and all kind of animals and they used spear for bear—also harpoon spear. They used it for seal, oogruk and white whale. In summer time at Kotzebue, people from all villages, Noatak, Kobuk and Selawik, gather together at sealing point at Shesualik. When the weather was good clear and calm they went out with Kayak and skin boat and drive white whale to shallow water. When they get to shallow water about three or four feet deep they started to spear them with harpoon spear and kill them with spear.

Now today at Kotzebue they use outboard with skin boat and other power boat for hunting oogruk and white whale. No more paddle skin

They use bow arrow for deer, bear and all kind of animals.

11

They also use snare for deer, rabbit and ptarmigan.

Ahgupuk

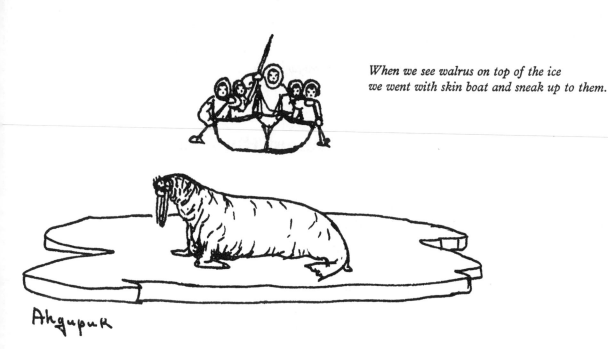

When we see walrus on top of the ice
we went with skin boat and sneak up to them.

Ahgupuk

boat or Kayak. (Skin boat name in Eskimo, is oomiak). But they still use harpoon spear with line today. In early day ago they sneak on them oogruk and seal when they layed on top of the ice. They sneak right close to them so they can spear them with harpoon spear with line.

That how they get these seals and oogruk early days ago before they got the gun. Also they make seal and oogruk net out of seal hide, and they use those net in winter time under the ice for seal and oogruk.

Whole year around those hair seal stayed in Arctic Ocean; they followed the ice. When ice went up north they follow the ice. In winter time when Arctic Ocean froze they come back. Also Oogruk do the same thing as seal does. But walrus they showed up in spring around June up in Arctic. They come through at Point Hope around first part of June.

Some time big herd of walrus get on top of the ice and lay, and some of them in water swimming. When we see walrus layed on top of the ice we went with skin boat and sneak up to them. When we get right close to them we start shooting and as soon we had room enough for our skin boat on the ice where walrus lay, we pull up our boat on ice.

You got to watch close when you go after big herd of walrus like that. Watch along side of your skin boat where you were sitting for walrus to come up. Them walrus were danger when they were big herd like that. Sometime they come up and poke the skin boat and make hole on side of the boat. You got to watch pretty close when you go after Walrus. Walrus is good eating. Walrus stomack we use for our Eskimo drum skin.

In spring time there were more seal and oogruk than in winter. Seal and oogruk layed on top of the ice in spring time having sun bath. When you go after seal or oogruk on top of the ice, you got to sneak on them, don't let them see you. Them seal and oogruk watch pretty close when they layed on top of the ice. As soon as they see you they went right down in water. Seal and oogruk meat they good eating. Lot of white people around Nome and Kotzebue and some other place they like seal

Ahgupuk

You got to watch close when you go after walrus.
Sometime they come up and make hole in side of skin boat.

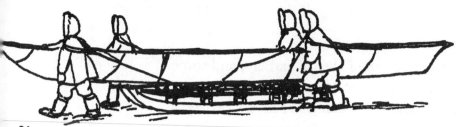

Hunters take oomiak (that skin boat) over ice on sled.

liver. Seal and oogruk have lot of blubber (that fat). That where we get our seal oil and from whale.

Every spring Kivalina and Noatak people they camp all along the coast for hunting with their family. Few family one place and so on. And all the men in same camp went out hunting with skin boat. Sometime two boat—sometime three boat—depend how many men they got. They divide crew among boat and owner of boat keep his crew during hunting. They keep hunting for oogruk and seal as long they got ice, when ice goes, they quit hunting.

Every time boat crew come home with catch they divide it among crew and everybody get some, and the woman had lot of work when hunter come home. Skin oogruk and cut up meat and hang up for dried meat—cut blubber for seal oil—put blubber in barrel or seal poke, and put seal oil in cold place. Hunters always have good time when they came home from hunting. They come to one place and have big dinner, every man's wife bring some thing to eat.

Eskimo make seal hook.
Use it to hook seal if he sink to bottom.

Ahgupuk

14

Bearded seal we call oogruk.
Not big like walrus but good meat.

When hunting for Oogruk and seal is over them hunter went to Kotzebue by boat with their family and dogs to trade their oogruk skin, seal skin, oogruk rope, seal rope, and seal oil. They traded with store or Noorvik people or Selawik people. After they spend their summer at Kotzebue they start back to their home.

Them people from Kobuk, Noorvik and Selawik—they spend their spring up the river for muskrat hunting. After rat hunting they come down to Kotzebue to meet coast seal hunter to get their oogruk skin, seal skin, oogruk or seal rope and seal oil for winter.

Woman had lot of work when hunter come home. Skin oogruk and cut up meat and hang up for dried meat.

15

6 Whaling Station Early Days Ago

FIRST whaling station at Point Hope was running by old man Cooper. They call that place Beacon Hill. Another whaling station was Jabber Town, about one-half mile towards Point Hope from Beacon Hill. There were Mr. Lieb, Tom George and Jim Allen, them are the old whalers that stayed at Jabber Town. From Beacon Hill it is 5 mile to Point Hope village. Point Hope Village is right at the Point, and Point Hope Mission is about one mile above village. Used to be a lot of people at church on Sunday when people went to church from Jabber Town, Beacon Hill and Point Hope.

Them whalers used to hire their men to work for them during whaling season. My father Taluk and my brother Johnnie used to have their

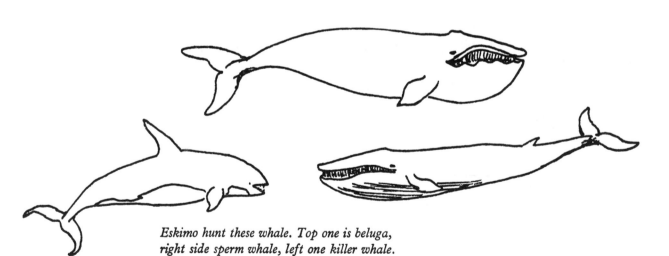

Eskimo hunt these whale. Top one is beluga, right side sperm whale, left one killer whale.

16

own crew for whaling. Whale bone was pretty high in those days, and lot of Point Hopers have their own whaling crew.

The kind of whale they go after is Bowhead whale at Point Hope. There were lot of white whale running too and lot of eider duck in spring at Point Hope.

If you want to get a good picture of the whaling go up in April and stay at Point Hope till June. First whale used to be showed up around April 10th or 12th and from there on till June. When walrus came through Point Hope that about the time whaling season is over.

In those day when them whaling station were at Jabber Town and Beacon Hill, they play foot ball against Point Hope. Sometime they get little rough in foot ball with men on both side. Women get played foot ball with men on both side. Women get rough like men do in foot ball games. Them Eskimo woman were pretty husky healthy woman early day ago. They drive dog team, went after wood and take care home— do everything.

How They Cut Bow-Head Whale   7

WHEN Eskimo caught whale they butchered on ice. They cut head off first, and they put sling on tail of the whale and meat same time while they pulling whale up. They used two set of block and tackle to pull whale up—when they get whale part ways up on ice that the time you should have your camera working. Also when woman started to cut piece of meat or piece of muktuk for themself for their own use, or for their family.

When they caught whale they always divided among the other skin boats. But first the boats owner divided the meat among his own boat's crew. There is lot of meat and muktuk out of one whale for whole village. They save everything out of the whale. They save skin out of whale lung and skin out of whale liver for their Eskimo drums.

When the cutting is over, they start to haul meat and muktuk under ground in their ice house for winter. And they took whale meat and muktuk and put it in poke or barrel and keep it in the house not cooked and put nothing with it. That meat and muktuk get sweet just like pickled. Everybody like it. I like it myself. It sure was good. Na-koo! (Na-koo mean good)

You know when they put meat and muktuk in barrel or seal poke they call it "mee-kee-gak."

They cut up whale and they took whale meat and muktuk and put it in poke or barrel for pickle.

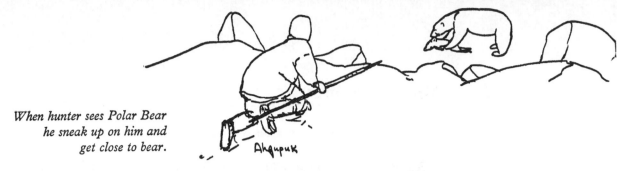

*When hunter sees Polar Bear
he sneak up on him and
get close to bear.*

Ahgupuk

About Polar Bear　　8

POLAR BEAR STAY on the ice. They live on seal and oogruk. Them Polar Bear they dangerous animals when they were hungry. They not afraid to come right to village when they hungry.

They go after anything, men or dog. But around November, female Polar Bear come up on the coast for breed. They get under snow bank and stayed till they born their cub, and come out around middle of March from under the snow bank with their young bear and started out to the ocean.

Sometime Eskimo find them just before they come out with their young bear, and kill the mother bear and raise the young bear. Keep them in the house, feed them, take them out day time, let them play out door.

Them Polar Bear had good fur in winter time. Eskimo hunt them in winter time. When hunter sees Polar Bear he sneak up on him and get close to bear so he can have good chance to shoot. Sometime when Polar Bear sees men they start to run away from him and the hunter start run after Polar Bear. Sometime hunter caught up with Polar Bear and kill the bear. Polar Bear had good meat. Polar Bear live mostly on seal blubber and oogruk blubber. They eat more blubber than they do meat.

WHEN I BECAME a young man there was no caribou on the coast. Sometime trappers get caribou way up inland. My mother use to tell us there were lot of caribou when she was a little girl right on the coast and later they disappear.

After I quit school, I used to go trapping with my brother Johnnie Kopatkok with dog team. We went way up inland over divide to Koo-pa-roak river. We carried our dog feed with us, we never see any caribou on trail

Later I went with reindeer team. So once a while we start seeing caribou. Every year caribou seem to be getting more and more where we used to be trapping and caribou getting closer to the coast every year. Now today caribou is right close to the beach in Arctic. In summer they right on the coast.

There is good mountain sheep range at Kivalina south river. No danger—easy to climb pretty close to the head of Kivalina river. And there are lot of big brown bear close to head of Kukpuk River.

There is good mountain sheep range at Kivalina south river. No danger, easy to climb.

One time there were four of us around the head of Kukpuk River. When we wake in the morning we saw one brown bear, right after we drink our coffee we saw another bear. As we left from our camp we saw three more brown bear. We did not bother them because we long ways from home.

And there is six or seven igloo right on top of the high mountain. Nobody know anything about them igloo. Not even was told in stories. Those igloo that was top on the mountain—was never been found yet by those man that work for museum. You can see long ways around from the top of that mountain.

White Fox 10

WHITE FOX live on the ice like Polar Bear but them come on land for breed. When trapping season open we used to trap them white fox out on the ice and we use just the seal blubber for bait. On land we use fish and squirrel for bait and chop bait very fine around trap. That how we trap foxes. We trap for red fox on land, same as we do for white fox. Use fish and squirrel for bait. Red fox stay on land, also cross fox and silver.

Sometime we track fox. We followed fox by his track with snow shoe, and when we get up to the fox we shoot them with our rifle. We general used 30-30, 25-35, and .303 rifle for foxes and polar bear and brown bear. We used them kind of gun for all kind of animals in Arctic of Alaska.

Now today caribou is right close to the beach in Arctic. In summer we get them right on the coast.

11 About Muskrat Hunt

FIRST time when I went hunting for muskrat I don't know anything about hunting muskrat. I went back of Kotzebue and go around them lake. I caught few muskrat and it was getting late. I went down to a lake where I saw two muskrat, I caught them both of them.

I stop in that lake about two hours, waiting for another muskrat to come up and I make cup of tea some time. But nothing showed up. I skin them two muskrat and hang the meat on willow to pick them up on my way back. Clean the guts out same time. While I was waiting for muskrat another hunter showed up. He came over to me, it was John Sheffer and we stay there for awhile, finally he ask me to go way up with him.

I said, "Okay, let's go." So we start together—we came to a lake— we saw one muskrat. John caught it with his 22 rifle. Only one we see in that lake, so we keep moving. Farther up we saw another muskrat. John told me go and give a shot at that muskrat. So I just get little closer to muskrat. I start aim my gun.

I got right close to muskrat and I shot muskrat.

John said to me, "That too far, Paul, you might miss it." And John said to me, "You can walk right close to muskrat as long you don't make noise when muskrat resting on top grass or ice."

So I start walk up to muskrat. I walk up slow, John watch me so I got right close to muskrat and I shot muskrat little way and I got it.

John Sheffer taught me—right there good lesson how to hunt muskrat.

Their meat is good to eat, it better yet after you take the skin off and take the guts out and let it hang for day or so and cook it and then you have good meat to eat.

That night till morning we caught few muskrat. When the sun get hot, about eight in the morning, we went to sleep and sleep till five at evening. When we wake up we have our breakfast, after breakfast we left again and hunt whole night for muskrat.

I start to use a gun since I was 7 year old. First gun I remember my father bought for me it was 22 short single shot. I caught my first ptarmigan with that 22 short rifle. And my mother put up big party in our camp for all people in our camp. My mother make Eskimo ice cream and berries and all kind of food to eat. Everybody enjoy to eat my first ptarmigan party.

In early day ago them parents when their son caught any kind of bird or seal or fox or deer, they used to put up party for the first catch their son caught. That what my parents do on every games I caught— first catch they put up party—big feast—for all their friends.

I start to use gun since I was seven year old.
I caught ptarmigan and my mother put up big party.

Ahgupuk

12   Making Oomiak and Kayak

PAPA Eskimo call big skin boat oomiak and little skin boat kayak. Early days ago our old folk never use hickory for making sled or skin boat. People at Kotzebue, Kivalina, Noatak and Point Hope get their skin boat frame and Kayak frame from forest. There are forests up the Noatak and Kobuk rivers from Kotzebue village. You could see forest as far you could see across Kotzebue bay. You can get all the wood you want and float them down the river in summer time to Kotzebue.

In winter time some people used to go up to Noatak river with dog team and cut timber for skin boat frames and kayak frames and haul it with dog team. People in Arctic of Alaska they build their skin boat frame from spruce tree or birch. People from Point Hope and Kivalina get their timber from Noatak river for frame.

Our old Eskimo build their skin boat and kayak frame almost like Diomede and King Island. But our old folk use oogruk skin to cover their skin boat. And they use seal skin to cover their kayak. Diomede and King Islander—they use walrus skin to cover oomiak and oogruk skin (bearded seal) to cover their kayak. But in Arctic of Alaska the kayak was made altogether different from Diomede and King Islanders. Them kayak in Arctic of Alaska smaller than Diomede or King Islander.

When Selawik people went to Kotzebue in summer they bring these birch tree with them and trade them to people at Kotzebue that came from Noatak or Kivalina. Depend on weather in early days when they

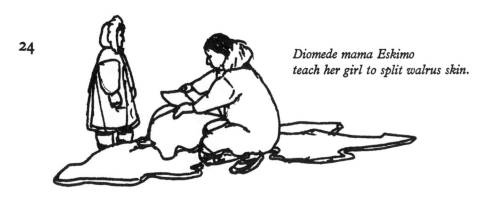

Diomede mama Eskimo
teach her girl to split walrus skin.

travel with skin boat. When the sea get too rough they just made a camp on beach and start off again when it calm down. They never travel in real rough sea with them skin boat in early days, unless they were get caught in bay like in Kotzebue sound and they travel rough sea to make it to other side.

Oomiak big open boat, seven, eight feet wide—maybe thirty feet long. Depend. Hold lots of people. These kayak was made for one man to use in water, same as little boat. They use them kayak for hunting and fishing, they use them for anything. These kayak pretty narrow and they real long.

We take these kayak on sled in winter time when we went out hunting seal. We use dog team in winter time for hunting and came home with full load of seal. Sometimes we don't get anything, sometime we get all we want.

Diomede mama Eskimo teach her girl to split walrus skin; make two skins. Walrus hide real tough. Inside skin use for cover oomiak. Inside skin dry tough, and it waterproof. After skin dry, woman wet up skin little bit and sew skin together for cover of skin boat. Sew real fast so all get sewed together while still wet, then when dry again all skin watertight. It take several skin to cover one oomiak.

Papa Eskimo teach his boy how to spread skin—all sewed together—out flat on grass in front of skin boat frame, then pull up skin and lash over front of frame. Then all these Eskimo men push frame on hide until pull tight and pull up skin all over frame and fasten frame with seal rope.

I think very few Eskimo boy today would make sled, snowshoe, oomiak and kayak. Now today I think not many Eskimo girl learn how to split walrus hide any more. It become lost art.

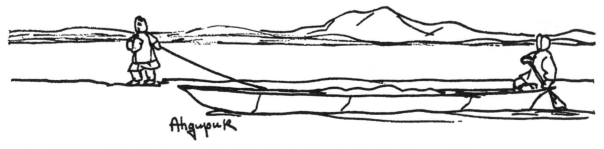

Papa Eskimo call big skin boat oomiak, little skin boat kayak. Use them for everything.

13 Shea Fish at Kotzebue

IN THE fall after the Kotzebue bay freeze up, Kotzebue boys put net under the ice. They having their net whole year around for shea fish and get lot of fresh fish. Shea fish taste almost like halibut and is white same as halibut meat—white. And around in March they start to get them shea fish with hook in Kotzebue bay. They fish till ice is dangerous to travel on. When they start fishing for shea fish you could see people every place.

It lot of fun to get shea fish with hook. You would enjoy hooking for shea fish in spring time on top the ice. Make coffee once in while—sun is warm—you would have lot of fun. I saw a shea fish a fellow brought in one time to a store—it weigh 54 #. You know they pretty good size fish. When you get one shea fish you have meat there for two or three days. They do the hooking for shea fish above Kotzebue town in spring. They went up with dog team, take tent, sleeping bag and grub with them and make camp on the ice. When a person hit right spot it never take long to get sled load of shea fish with hook.

Kotzebue boys put net under ice, catch shea fish.
They fish till ice is dangerous to travel on.

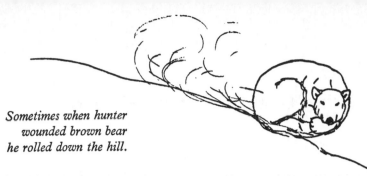

Sometimes when hunter
wounded brown bear
he rolled down the hill.

One time at Kotzebue I went up fishing for shea fish in spring and we seen a fellow hit a right spot as soon as he throw his hook in hole and as soon as line stretch another fish bite. He was going all day like that. We get around him make hole in the ice and hooking—we did get some all right but we did not do like him. Oh Boy! that man get lot of fish in no time. His name was Charlie Kenworthy.

Brown Bear   14

WE WAS trained by our old folk how to hunt game in the Arctic of Alaska. My father used to tell me when I was a kid, if I ever hunt brown bear, if the bear lay on side of the mountain, go over from top side.

He said some time when hunter wounded bear he roll down the hill, get roll up like ball and roll down. So I saw bear one time roll down the hill side after the boy wounded him. He get roll up like a ball and roll down the hill side. Go fast too.

Them brown bear get plenty fat in the fall before they get in their hole for winter. They stay in their hole all winter and come out in spring. Squirrels do same thing as brown bear. Stay in their hole for winter, come out in spring.

AROUND 1945 I work for U.S.E.D. (U.S. Engineering Department) at Nome and there were a lot of new comers from States that were there on first trip to Alaska. At evening when we get through working, after supper them white men and some ladies used to came down to our camp and spent their evening with us and asking me about the Eskimo in Arctic of Alaska. They told me why the question they ask, they said they read it from the book that book writers from States come to Alaska and write about Arctic.

I told them I read some of them books that book writers wrote in the States after they made trip to Alaska. I told them some things true— lot of them wasn't true about us Eskimo of Arctic of Alaska. When them book writer get to Alaska they never tried to find out how the Eskimo make living in Arctic of Alaska—they just went to white people home and tried to find out from them white people how those Eskimo make living in Arctic.

One evening one of the white men ask me did we use seal oil for bath? And I turn around and ask him, before I answer his question, I said to him, did he ever use Wesson Oil for bath? He said, "No!" And I said to him, what he use for bath? He said, he use soap and water, and I said to him, "That what we use, soap and water."

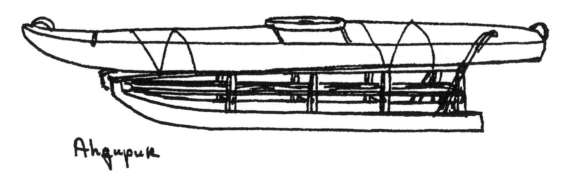

Ahgupuk

Eskimo Legend, Boy and Jade Ax   16

ONCE UPON a time there were old lady and her grandson living. Her grandson ask his grandmother lot of time if she knew any village close by but grandmother always told her grandson same story all time, that she never knew anybody close by.

Everytime when grandson play out door he saw a lonely tree standing by their small igloo. His grandmother always told him not to bother that tree.

So one time when the boy play out he was thinking, "Why did grandma always told me to not to bother that tree?" So he went home and get his small jade ax and chop the tree down.

After he cut the tree he went in and he saw his grandma chop in two. So he went back to the tree and put the tree together. After put tree together he went home where he saw grandma twisting sinew for thread!

Eskimo True Story, Nice Good Looking Lady   17

ONCE UPON a time there were family had a daughter at Point Hope. Their daughter become nice looking lady. When their daughter became lady, nice looking young men from Point Hope or different village visit this nice looking lady, and ask her to become wife but this lady always refuse them. Not really refuse them, but she always told them if they were better Eskimo dancer than her, she will become wife to best Eskimo dancer.

29

Boy get his small jade ax and he chop that tree down.

Ahgupuk

One time one of the young men come over to see her. He had needle case with him made out of ivory. This nice young good looking lady had her own home by that time then, and the young man come into her home. When young man come in lady saw needle case. Gee, it look good to her.

She said to young man, "What you got there with you? I want to see it."

Young man gave it to her. Lady got hold of it, look it over—the needle case.

She said, "Gee, this look good to me. I like it, suppose we get together and become wife and husband and went out whaling this spring and caught whale and put up big feast. After big feast and Na-lee-ka-tuk (blanket toss game) we have dance. I wonder how we look like when we dance together."

They both start dancing and after they get through dancing lady turn around to this young man and she said, "I'm not going to become your wife because you not much of Eskimo dancer."

After big feast and Na-lee-ka-tuk we have dance.

Ahgupuk

And the lady took needle case—let the young man go.

Few days after another young man come to see this lady. This time young man had lady knife (oo-loo—that the name for woman knife). When young man came in lady saw lady knife; and lady ask young man just like she did not know what the man got. Young man gave it to her. Lady got hold of it, she was surprise to see lady knife.

The lady say, "I was hoping long time to have lady knife made, so I got it now. Suppose we get together, become wife and husband and went out whaling this spring and caught whale, and after whaling we put up big feast for all people at Point Hope. After feast we had Na-lee-ka-tuk, and dance. I wonder how we look like when we do Eskimo dance together."

So they started Eskimo dance. After they dance lady turn around and face young man and said to him, "I'm sorry. I not going to become your wife because you don't know how to do Eskimo dance."

So the lady took the knife and let the young man go.

Third young man was a poor boy, he got no parents, just grandpa. So this poor boy take a visit to this nice looking young lady. But he was poor boy, nothing to take with him, so he took sinew with him. When he came into this lady home he hide them sinew. When poor boy came in lady saw him and she ask him what he got with him. Poor boy did not tell her. But the lady keep asking him, so the poor boy told her what he brought her. Lady was very please for them sinew. She have them in her hand for long while.

Eskimo lady say to poor boy, "After whaling is over I make you fancy mukluk also for myself—I will use these sinew. Then we will have big feast for all people at Point Hope. After we caught whale at spring time, and we have Na-lee-ka-tuk and Eskimo dance. I was just wonder

*Nice looking young lady sit down
on the floor and start sewing.*

how pair of us look like when we dance together."

So they start Eskimo dance. After they through with first dance she said to poor boy, "let us do it again."

So they start dance again. After they get through with last Eskimo dance she turn around to this poor boy.

She said, "You nearly got me this time but you didn't make it."

And the poor boy turn to her, "I am going to tell my grandpa!" he say, and run out.

After poor boy went out nice looking young lady sit down on top of deer skin on the floor and start sewing. While she was sewing she heard something. It get closer every time when finally she hear it clearly. It was poor boys grandpa.

Old man was saying, "It was me, poor boys grandpa. You was refusing them nice looking young men and good hunter for these years. So I am going to have you for myself."

And the nice good looking lady got mad, tried to get up, but she can't move. She was paralyzed. Finally old man show up—coming up to nice looking lady—walking on hand and knee, he got too old, can't stand on his feet. But the nice looking lady become his wife. None of the young men like her anymore.

32

BEFORE WHITE PEOPLE come to Alaska Eskimo don't know anything about white people foods. In early days ago Eskimo never drink coffee or tea or whisky. Don't even know how bread look like. Before white come to Alaska, Eskimo live on meat and berries and they use boiling water off meat for coffee and tea. They eat their meat with seal oil, also they use seal oil for berries.

Them Eskimo before white people come they were healthy people, not like us Eskimo today. Them Eskimo woman early days ago they pickled all kind of berries and willow leaf and put them away for winter.

In spring time men do the hunting for seal and oogruk and in summer hunting for caribou. They saved all the meat. Woman dried up seal and oogruk meat and caribou meat and put them in seal poke with seal oil and put them away for winter. Also woman do the fishing in summertime, dried up fish—and put them away for winter.

Eskimo people who stayed up the river they do the fishing whole year round. They put fish trap with willow in the river. Like on Noatak River and some other rivers. They get lot of fish in winter.

Them Eskimo early days ago they never buy meat, they get it themself. They been getting wild games for food for whole year around. They hunt for it because they don't raise cattle or pigs like white people and in winter time they like frozen fish and caribou meat or seal meat or oogruk meat with seal oil.

They eat them frozen. They never eat them when they thaw or they never touch cattle meat or pigs for frozen meat to eat, because they

33

*Early days ago,
Eskimos catch tomcod
through hole in ice.
Still do.*

were raise in farm. They like wild animals for food.

In winter time when they travel even on the trail when they stop for lunch they had frozen meat. That frozen meat will warm you up in no time, after you eat it. Eskimo in the Arctic sure like to have frozen meat in winter time. Also like to have black whale muktuk and whale meat.

Now today we used cattle meat or lamb meat, any kind of meat, that raise on farm. But we got to cook them first and put salt and pepper and onion to taste with.

When we was at Point Hope we used to go egging with small skin boat in spring time around first part of July and then we come back home with full load of eggs. And then we have eggs for long while. They keep good. Them sea birds eggs,—one egg is size of two chicken eggs.

The beach is sandy along the coast all the way up to Point Barrow. There were two big capes full of sea birds—one this side of Point Hope and one the other side of Point Hope.

We used to climb them cliffs to get sea birds eggs.

We used to climb cliff to get them eggs—sometime we climb pretty high. Sometime we use rope on the danger part. And we keep them eggs in cool place. They last long time.

Sometime woman come along when we went for egging, as a cook, and they get their share of eggs when we divided the eggs what we got among us boys that went for egging in one boat. We divided equal share to everybody.

Rubbing Nose Kiss   19

I THINK OLD ESKIMO has a better way of kissing their friends or their girl friend in early days ago. Because we could tell it by the way our old people tell us. They used to tell us there were hardly any T.B. case in early days ago among Eskimo. Our old folk used to tell us they were told from their old generation to watch for anybody that got T.B., to watch the dishes the person use. Old Eskimo watch pretty close this T.B. case from their old generation, way before white people come to Alaska.

I think that why our old Eskimo rubbing their nose for kiss, so they won't spread T.B. germ among themself. Now we younger generation

Our old Eskimo had a better way of kissing their friends or girl friends.

learn our kisses from white people and just forget about our old generation Eskimo rubbing nose kiss. We think it better way to kiss with lip instead of rubbing nose. Now today we been kissing our friends or our girl friends with our lips like white people, because that are the one more thing we learn from our friends the white people.

Now today we know we been spreading this T.B. germ among our friends or to our girl friends or to our boy friend by kissing with our lips.

Now today we had more T.B. cases among our Eskimo than we do in early days ago. I think our old Eskimo know better than we do today. Our old Eskimo they were healthy, strong and live longer in their days, than we do today.

20 To-Va-Ka-Nok

ONCE UPON A TIME there were two boys, Mok-toy-ok and Pan-u-tak, growing up together in the village of Wales on Cape Prince of Wales. (Eskimo name of village is Kee-gni-gin.) These boys play together and never get far apart. They call each other To-va-ka-nok. (This mean partner.)

One of them boy, Mok-toy-ok, tell his partner "When we become man we will get one woman for our wife." The other boy say "Yes." They promise each other they will stay together in same igloo, they will build igloo for themself when they become a man, and get one wife. Otherwise, they said to each other, if they each get a wife they might get separate apart.

So when they become men, they build their igloo and stay together in igloo for long time.

One evening, kind of getting late, Mok-toy-ok went out and never came in for awhile. Finally, he came in and brought a woman with him. Pan-u-tak had never seen this woman before, she was not from their village of Wales. So Pan-u-tak said "Well, partner, you finally get us a wife! This lady is nice looking lady. Now, partner, is this lady going to be wife for both of us?"

Mok-toy-ok never say a word for a while, he thinking. Finely, he said to his partner, "Well, partner, I think this lady is for myself alone."

"Well, what wrong?" asked Pan-u-tak. "You always tell me when we growing up, when we become man we build igloo and we get one wife," and that woman not saying one word. "Now we build our igloo and stay together and now you find us a wife. How come you want to have that woman for yourself alone?"

Mok-toy-ok said "I've changed my mind. I'll have this woman for myself alone."

"Well, partner, where did you get this woman? You think you can show me where you get her?" ask Pan-u-tak.

"Why yes. Sure. I'll show you where I got this lady. When you went out from our igloo, you walk right straight ahead till you find old Eskimo drum been broke one side. When you look through that broken side you will see ladies picking berries. If you see one right under you, try and see if you can make her look up. If she look up at you, you told her you want her to come up. But be sure you don't went down, even if she told you to come down!" Pan-u-tak say, "Okey," to his partner, and went out.

37

When you look through that broken drum you will see ladies picking berries.

When he went out, he walk straight ahead until he find old Eskimo drum one side broken out like he was told by his partner. He look down through that broken side and see ladies picking berries. There was one lady right below him. He made noise to see if he could get this lady to look up.

Sure enough, lady look up and saw him, and young man get good look at lady. Gee, that lady sure look pretty, and the young man say to lady, "I'm looking for lady for my wife. You will have nice home, have everything you want." But the lady said, "You come down here, instead of me coming up there to you. I got no brother; I'm the only one in family. My parents will be glad to have you. I never been belong to any man yet. I will take you home to my parent."

So Pan-u-tak went with the young lady.

Mok-toy-ok waiting at Wales for his partner to come back but his partner did not come back. Mok-toy-ok went out and look for that broken drum but the drum was gone. So he went all over the village to see if he could find his partner, but could not find him anywhere.

So Pan-u-tak went with the young lady.

Now, at Kotzebue (this was happen in the fall time), the people at Kotzebue village hear that one of the berry pickers bring home young man. They don't know where this young man come from so Kotzebue people kill Pan-u-tak.

Now Mok-toy-ok stay at Wales all winter. One day stranger came from different village, from Shishmaref. Mok-toy-ok sent his wife to ask stranger to come to their igloo to eat. After eat Mok-toy-ok ask him if he hear anything from different village about Pan-u-tak. This man tell Mok-toy-ok they hear from Kotzebue this fall that one of the women that pick berries brought young man home. When Kotzebue find out, they kill young man.

When Mok-toy-ok hear this, he sure that was his partner. He thank the Shishmaref man for the news, and hitch up his dogs and leave for Kotzebue.

When he got to Kotzebue it was night; and he went right on back of Kotzebue and look over them dead body that been dead this fall. (In those days they just wrap dead person with skin.) He went from one dead person to another until he finally found his partner. After he find Pan-u-tak, he wrap him up nicely and weep over him and put him away good.

Mok-toy-ok pretty mad. He went down to first igloo where every body asleep. When he went in he pull out his knife and kill every one in that igloo, women and all. Then he went into the next igloo and did the same thing. But one of them persons get away and get to next igloo. So Mok-toy-ok ran away in dark and went back to Wales. Wales Eskimo name Kee-gni-gin. And the Kotzebue people didn't know who the man was until long time later when Mok-toy-ok die and his wife come back to Kotzebuc and tell who it was. Kotzebue Eskimo name Ke-ke-ta-ro-ak.

21 Ah-Pa-Kee-Na

ONCE UPON A TIME there was a man name Ah-pa-kee-na. He had a wife, also both of his parents living.

He was a great hunter at Point Hope. Every spring he caught whale. Never miss a spring. So in fall time they were using kayak to hunt seal or oogruk. They using harpoon for seal and oogruk those days, no gun.

So one fall Ah-pa-kee-na was hunting. While he was hunting way out, young ice came right along the beach and Ah-pa-kee-na could not make it to shore and Ah-pa-kee-na get lost. Never come home. So Ah-pa-kee-na wife become widow.

Once in a while she came with whale meat and muktuk to Ah-pa-kee-na parent.

Old lady jump up and grab bucket and pour right onto her son.

40

Finely, Ah-pa-kee-na mother notice water was gone in their water bucket also some meat was gone. She told her husband what she find out and next night old man start watch. He went to bed and stay awake. Finely, he went fast a sleep. When he wake everything was gone—meat and water.

So next night he told his wife to put more meat and more water in bucket, so he told his wife to go to sleep as usual. So he himself lay in his bed same as usual. So he had something sharp in his hand to keep him wake. Everytime when he start to go to sleep when he hit his hand and hit that sharp edge stone in his hand he get quite awake every time.

Finely, draft coming in cold air and he quite awake then. Here he saw their son Ah-pa-kee-na come in. Old man didn't move—just watch his son what he would do. When Ah-pa-kee-na come in he get hold of that wooden dish with meat in it. He ate it all up and he get hold of that bucket and drink all up. After he eat and drink he went out.

When the old folk wake up in the morning he told his wife that he saw their son come in and eat and drink water. After he eat and drink he went out.

The old folk just wondering how they would get hold of their son. So old man told his wife every night when she put meat and water put them further in their igloo away from their door way. So the old lady doing what she was told from her old man. So the old man think if he jump on to his son Ah-pa-kee-na he could caught him. So every night when their son came in he watch him eat and drink. So old man think the best time to grab their son when he start drinking water from the bucket.

So next morning old man told his wife. They both will stay awake to-night. Old man said he going to grab his son tonight.

So his wife put out meat and water again same as usual. They both stayed awake and waiting. While they waiting both get sleepy, but as soon draft coming in both wake.

They both in bed as usual when they saw their son come in. Parents watch their son when he eat meat. When their son get through eating meat he grab bucket and start drinking from bucket. When he cover his face with bucket old man jump on him and grab their son. And old lady jump up same time and grab bucket and pour right on to her husband and son.

And old people got their son back and they got some skin and make room for their son inside their igloo.

They don't want people at Point Hope to know. So nobody at Point Hope know old folk got their son back. It was middle of the winter when they got their son back. Every once a while Ah-pa-kee-na wife come to old folks home, bring them some meat and muktuk that she save from her husband catch last spring.

One evening when she come in she told old folk there a man want to have her for his wife. And the old folk tell their daughter-in-law they will let her know to-morrow, and their daughter-in-law say "Okay."

When their daughter-in-law went out they talk to their son Ah-pa-kee-na. Their son told his parents it okay with him. Next day when their daughter-in-law came they told her it okay with them if she have that man for her husband and old man told his daughter-in-law they would went out whaling this spring—use her first husband Ah-pa-kee-na whaling outfit.

When whaling season open everybody got boat—start out for whaling. They caught few whale.

Also Ah-pa-kee-na wife with her new husband went out whaling with

42

Ah-pa-kee-na boat. But Ah-pa-kee-na boat did not get whale that spring.

When they get through whaling they start having big feast and blanket toss. Old man told his wife "Go over to son wife and ask her if she got any more clothing left of Ah-pa-kee-na; and if she have, told her I want two pair."

So old lady went over to their daughter-in-law. When old lady come in, their daughter-in-law ask her if she want anything.

Old lady say, "Yes." She said, "Old man want to have two pair set of new clothing from Ah-pa-kee-na clothing, if there any left."

Their daughter-in-law said, "Yes, there lot of them new clothing left. Nobody touch them."

Old lady take home two pair new clothing. (Ah-pa-kee-na never been out yet since his parents got hold of him. These old folks was waiting to take their son up to Kamatoak feast and blanket toss.)

So old man told his wife, "We wait till we see everybody go to feast and na-lee-ka-tuk" (Na-lee-ka-tuk is blanket toss.) "Then wait till they start blanket toss."

Finely, they start blanket toss. And old folks take their son from south side of the Point and went around point to north side, two men and one woman showing up from the north side, they walking up to blanket toss.

They were long ways when the people first saw them. Lot of people was wondering who they are. Finely, one of the Point Hope man, say, "Gee, that man in middle act and walk like Ah-pa-kee-na."

And one of the man said, "You think Ah-pa-kee-na live this long? He's gone long ago, you will never see a sign of Ah-pa-kee-na now."

*When whaling season open,
everybody got boat—
start out for whaling.*

Point Hope people stop blanket toss and watch them three person coming—two man and one woman. Finely, they come close. They were Ah-pa-kee-na himself and his father and mother.

As soon as Ah-pa-kee-na get to blanket toss he jump right in blanket (big walrus hide). And everybody was happy to see their great whaler come back alive. They sure did have great time.

Ah-pa-kee-na got his wife back and get another woman for that man. In next spring Ah-pa-kee-na and that man went out whaling in Ah-pa-kee-na boat, and they caught whale. From that time on Ah-pa-kee-na and that man they do whaling together every spring and they never miss. They caught whale every spring.

*Ah-pa-kee-na and that man
they do whaling together.
They caught whale every spring.*

Ahgupuk

IN EARLY DAYS AGO, Eskimo change wife in Arctic of Alaska to make big family and have lots of relatives. Suppose here, man and wife from Kotzebue and man and wife from Point Hope. Them men they exchange wife, they agree everything among them self, and they claim their children just like one family. And when them children grow up, parents told their children they have half brother or half sister at Point Hope or Kotzebue.

Then when them children grow up and meet together at Point Hope or Kotzebue they know each other by their parents name so they call each other half brother or half sister, treat each other like their own full brother or sister; and the parents treat all them children just like all their own children, calling them son or daughter.

In early days ago them Eskimo parents was proud to tell their children that they have half brother or half sister in that other village. They told their children to look them up when they went to that other village, also mention their parents name.

In early days ago many man made family and relatives for himself with some other man's wife. Suppose a man from Kivalina went to Point Barrow and meet a man and wife there. Them Barrow people invite this Kivalina man to their home and told him to stay with them. Then Kivalina man ask this Barrow man if he could have his wife, so their children will be like brother and sister. And when this man went home to Kivalina, he told his wife they have more family and relatives for their children at Barrow. And some times that Barrow man come to Kivalina and he visit with that man and his wife at Kivalina, then when he go home to Barrow he told his wife there that they have more family and relatives for their children at Kivalina!

That why old Eskimo change their wives in early days ago, to make more family and more relatives. And now today, Eskimo don't change with their wife. This been stop quite while back, when first mission get to Arctic of Alaska.

23 Ka-va-shook Makes Even

THERE was a man name Ka-va-shook got a wife and kids and he had one big dog and kept it like one of his kids. Ka-va-shook was a Shishmaref man. There was a few more families beside Ka-va-shook family. They have sod igloo in that place. In spring they stay in their winter home and do some hunting and put away some food in their ice house. In the summer they move away from their winter home.

Eskimo people were having ice house years and years before any white man come to Alaska, so they can save food. Put away some food in summer for winter.

This is how they made their ice house. They dig in ground, some of them way down, they mostly have around seven or eight feet down and put frame all around the hole and top cover it up with sod and mud. They had them hole around eight by ten or ten by ten that how they make their ice house for their food in summer, so their food won't be spoil in summer.

That spring Ka-va-shook was doing hunting and fishing, after he put away some food for winter for his kids in their ice house, Ka-va-shook wife was helping her husband drying meat and fish what her husband get. And then they left their winter home and go some place else and spent their summer.

Ka-va-shook wife and kids they were picking berries in seal poke with oil and save them to take home with them to their winter home. And fall come and freeze up and snow all over, then Ka-va-shook got home safely with his family to their winter home. After they got everything ready in their home, Ka-va-shook went over to their ice house to get a dried fish with oil in seal poke for his kids. When Ka-va-shook got in his ice house that seal poke with dried fish was gone.

He was just wondering who the person want to do that to him. Everybody know he need that dried fish in seal poke for his kids. Ka-va-shook got big family, he had hard time trying to keep his family. But lot of his own people was helping him to keep up his family. So Ka-va-shook went back to his wife and told his wife that seal poke of dried fish was gone in their ice house.

Ahgupuk

47

Eskimo people were having ice house
long before white man come,
so their food won't spoil in summer.

So Ka-va-shook went out from his home and went to his neighbor. When he went in to his neighbor Ka-va-shook ask them, "Did they know any body come to their village?" He said, "I miss one seal poke of my dried fish. It was gone from my ice house."

His neighbor said, "Yes, there was a man here yesterday and went home this morning. He got good size of seal poke in his sled. We don't find out what was in that seal poke. He must get that seal poke from your ice house."

Ka-va-shook said to his neighbor, "What that man name?"

And his neighbor say, "That man was here, his name was Ta-moo-gu-tay-luck."

So Ka-va-shook thank his neighbor and went home to his family. When he got home he told his wife that Ta-moo-gu-tay-luck got his poke of dried fish.

So early next morning Ka-va-shook wake up and start to Ta-moo-gu-tay-luck village. When Ka-va-shook get to Ta-moo-gu-tay-luck village, he stop with one of the family he know in that village. When he went in there was a man and his wife in igloo. Ka-va-shook told them what was happen in his village in a day when he got home to his winter village and what he miss in his ice house. And the man and his wife told Ka-va-shook they saw Ta-moo-gu-tay-luck yesterday when he came home, he got big seal poke on his sled.

"So that was yours," they said. "That Ta-moo-gu-tay-luck is funny man. He tried to get best of any body he know. He think he is something of himself and everybody know him, he is husky guy, good runner, good jumper and good for everything and he is stuck up guy, too. Don't care for anybody else, he just want to have everything for himself instead somebody else have it. That the kind of guy he is."

48

Now this man Ka-va-shook he's not stuck up guy, just willing to help anybody with what he got. And did not be proud of himself. Nobody don't know whether he's good runner or good jumper like Ta-moo-gu-tay-luck, nobody know except Ka-va-shook himself.

Then Ka-va-shook told man and his wife, "If Ta-moo-gu-tay-luck miss anything in the morning, just told him I was around and got it and took it home with me for my own use."

Ta-moo-gu-tay-luck did not know Ka-va-shook was in their village that day. So Ta-moo-gu-tay-luck wake his wife early in that morning to have his breakfast ready so after he ate his breakfast Ta-moo-gu-tay-luck went out and go up to his cache to get his seal net, he was going out to put seal net that morning. But everything was gone, seal net, ice pick, everything that goes with seal net. He don't know what to do for while. Everybody sleeping. He went back to his igloo and told his wife, "That seal net and rest of the stuff that goes with seal net is gone!"

Ka-va-shook was doing fishing. Ka-va-shook wife was drying what fish her husband get.

49

Ahgupuk

When their neighbor wake up Ta-moo-gu-tay-luck went over and told them what was happen. He said his seal net and the rest of the stuff that goes with seal net was gone from his cache. He said he miss them this morning. And his neighbor told Ta-moo-gu-tay-luck,

"Ka-va-shook was around last night. Ka-va-shook told us if you ever miss anything that he got it and took it home with him. He must have your seal net and the rest of the stuff that goes with net."

Gee, Ta-moo-gu-tay-luck jump up and said, "Do I have to let Ka-va-shook doing that to me? Taken my stuff from me without notify me?"

And his neighbor said, "You started it first. You went over to his place and went in to his ice house and take seal poke of some kind of meat and take it home with you. So Ka-va-shook wanted to make even with you so he took your seal net and take it home with him."

So Ta-moo-gu-tay-luck went out from his neighbor and went home. When he got home he told his wife, "I'm going over to Ka-va-shook village and see what I get from Ka-va-shook."

So Ta-moo-gu-tay-luck went over to Ka-va-shook village and got there just before dark, and Ta-moo-gu-tay-luck stay with Ka-va-shook neighbor.

When it got dark Ka-va-shook let his dog out for while. But his dog never come back. So Ka-va-shook went out and look for his dog, but he could not find his dog nowhere.

His neighbor told Ka-va-shook, "There were Ta-moo-gu-tay-luck around tonight. He must got your dog and took him home with him. Ta-moo-gu-tay-luck was with us tonight and he went out and disappear. Never come back. While he was here he was telling us why he let that female dog start robbing him of his stuff."

His neighbor told Ka-va-shook, "That Ta-moo-gu-tay-luck was call-

50

Both men were shooting at each other for quite awhile. Getting closer to each other every time.

Ahgupuk

ing you female dog."

Ka-va-shook jump up and said, "Female dog got no more life in him. He is going over to Ta-moo-gu-tay-luck village and fight him with bow and arrow."

So next morning Ka-va-shook left with sled and took walrus skin along. He told people that walrus skin will be his cover when Ta-moo-gu-tay-luck kill him.

Ka-va-shook got to Ta-moo-gu-tay-luck village and he stop same place where he stop when he first came. And Ka-va-shook told the man female dog came over to fight with Ta-moo-gu-tay-luck. "Will you go and tell Ta-moo-gu-tay-luck like that?"

And the man said, "I sure will go." And the man went over to Ta-moo-gu-tay-luck and told him, "There is female dog came over and want to fight with you and get over with trouble."

And this Ta-moo-gu-tay-luck notice it right away it was Ka-va-shook that he's calling female dog. Ta-moo-gu-tay-luck tell the man, "It getting late tonight but we sure will have fight early in the morning."

So everybody in the village find out there were going to be a fight between Ka-va-shook and Ta-moo-gu-tay-luck in early morning with bow and arrow.

51

So early in the morning when it get day light everybody in the village went out and get to the back of their village. They were waiting for Ka-va-shook and Ta-moo-gu-tay-luck to come out from igloo they were in. Finely, Ka-va-shook come out from igloo where he was and he coming up to the people. He had big long (female) parkie on.

Now they waiting for Ta-moo-gu-tay-luck. Finely he show up. It did not take long for Ta-moo-gu-tay-luck to come up to the people where they were standing. When Ta-moo-gu-tay-luck got close Ka-va-shook take off his long parkie. And the people was watching Ka-va-shook and Ta-moo-gu-tay-luck.

Ka-va-shook told Ta-moo-gu-tay-luck, "You shoot me first with bow and arrow."

But To-moo-gu-tay-luck told Ka-va-shook, "I did not start this fight first. Go ahead and start shoot first."

So Ka-va-shook start shoot first—he don't get even near Ta-moo-gu-tay-luck with arrow. So Ta-moo-gu-tay-luck shoot Ka-va-shook. He did the same thing, not get near Ka-va-shook. So both man were shooting each other for quite a while and miss each other. They were getting closer to each other every time so one time Ta-moo-gu-tay-luck shoot Ka-va-shook. Ka-va-shook jump side way and grab Ta-moo-gu-tay-luck arrow while it was fly.

And then Ka-va-shook use same arrow that he grab and he shoot and got Ta-moo-gu-tay-luck on his left arm that holding bow and Ta-moo-gu-tay-luck drop his bow on the ground. From then on Ka-va-shook been hitting Ta-moo-gu-tay-luck every shot he make with bow and arrow. Finely, Ta-moo-gu-tay-luck fell over and died.

Ka-va-shook turn to the people and say, "Is there anybody else want to fight with me?"

52

Nobody say a word except there was a man get forward and said to Ka-va-shook, "If I was in good shape like you, I would fight with you."

This man got bum ankle.

So Ka-va-shook just went down to the igloo where he was stayed and get his sled down from cache and get his dog. Also get that seal poke of dried fish. Ka-va-shook got everything back what Ta-moo-gu-tay-luck got from him and left for home. So Ka-va-shook got home safe to his family. His wife and kids were so glad to see their daddy back home safe.

Ka-va-shook surprise everybody in Ta-moo-gu-tay-luck village and in his own village. They thought Ka-va-shook was going to be killed by Ta-moo-gu-tay-luck. But Ka-va-shook kill Ta-moo-gu-tay-luck instead been killed, so Ka-va-shook been doing hunting at his home village. Put out net for seal under the ice and caught seal with the net he took away from Ta-moo-gu-tay-luck.

That day when Ka-va-shook left for home, Ta-moo-gu-tay-luck wife hire that man with bum ankle to have her husband come back to life again. That man with bum ankle was a medicine man. So that man work on Ta-moo-gu-tay-luck. Take all the arrows out and have Ta-moo-gu-tay-luck back to life again. And the medicine man told Ta-moo-gu-tay-luck not to eat any berries and leaves that been pick last summer and keep in ice house.

*Ka-va-shook go to **Ta-moo-gu-tay-luck** cache and get his seal poke of dried fish.*

Ahgupuk

"You can start eating berries and leaves when they grow this coming summer. You can eat all you want. You can eat anything now except berries and leaves. Don't touch anything that grow on the ground until this summer, when they grow themself again." That what man with bum ankle tell Ta-moo-gu-tay-luck.

So one day Ka-va-shook have stranger arrived from Ta-moo-gu-tay-luck village, that man bring news to Ka-va-shook from Ta-moo-gu-tay-luck. The news was saying next year about the same day when Ta-moo-gu-tay-luck and Ka-va-shook fight, Ta-moo-gu-tay-luck was coming over and fight with Ka-va-shook in Ka-va-shook village.

So Ta-moo-gu-tay-luck was okay. He was hunting and doing everything same as before and the summer getting close. Once a while he ask his wife if he could have some berries. But his wife always told him he got to wait till the berries grow on the ground. Then he will have all the berries he want. So his wife always talk her husband out.

But one time Ta-moo-gu-tay-luck go after his wife pretty hard. Beat her up and everything, and told her, why she stingy about berries?

Wife try to make her husband wait. Husband won't wait. Even his wife told her husband, "That medicine man told you to wait till berries grow itself from the ground. You can have all you want then. Why don't you wait? It won't be long now when berries grow."

But Ta-moo-gu-tay-luck can't wait any more. He wanted to eat berries right now. So his wife get some berries and leaves. Ta-moo-gu-tay-luck start eating berries and leaves and break his rule from his medicine man. Ta-moo-gu-tay-luck eat lot of berries and leaves.

After he eat, wife and husband went to bed. While they sleep Mrs. Ta-moo-gu-tay-luck wake up, her side getting sweat that been touch her husband. She wipe her side with her hand and look at her hand. Gee!

54

Her hand was bloody! Her husband was bleeding.

She get up quick and went over to their medicine man and told their medicine man what happen. And their medicine man just told the lady, "Just let your husband go." Medicine man said, "I heal him once and gave him rule so he break the rule. No use to help a man like that. Just let him die, better for him."

So when summer come Ka-va-shook hear Ta-moo-gu-tay-luck just died.

Eskimo Drum   24

OUR ESKIMO DRUM made out of hardwood nowadays. We only put skin on one side, and beat from other side. We use walrus stomach for our drum skin, or whale liver skin or whale lung skin.

Woman or man do lot of work on them drum skin before they get ready for use. We put skin on drum frame and use string to fasten skin to frame. We stretch that drum skin tight and put string around same time. We stretch the skin while it wet, and we keep it wet when we use in dance. We always use water when we use them drum, make sound better with stick.

When you see Eskimo dance you must be thinking it pretty hard work; but it not hard work, because we get used to it. It just like fox trot.

You know my friend, the reason why we use glove when we doing Eskimo dance? From the beginning, in every Eskimo dance man using glove, for being good manners they cover their hand with glove when they get in front of lot people.

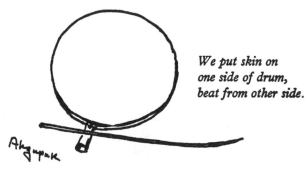

We put skin on one side of drum, beat from other side.

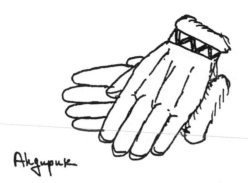

Ahgupuk

You know, my friend, it lot of fun to watch Eskimo dance. In this motion dance it better to have two or three man together in motion dance. Sometime we had two man and one woman. Some time two woman and one man. We had all kind of motion we put in dances. Hunting motion dance—Bow and arrow motion dance—rye whiskey motion dance—Joe Louis Fight motion dance—welcome motion dances —oh we had all kind of motion dances to enjoy the people that watch Eskimo dance. This wolf dance was started by Kotzebue dancers long long ago. This wolf dancing drum (it wooden drum) was found by a man that drifted in Arctic Ocean. This is the way it was found.

A man went out with Kayak in spring time, hunting oogruk on top of the ice. He sneak up on that oogruk with harpoon spear, and he harpoon oogruk and caught it. After he caught it, he went back to his kayak. His kayak was gone. Ice break off where his Kayak been. He don't know what to do. He was way out—maybe stay on that ice cake floating—never see land anymore. Every day that ice cake getting smaller, melting off. Lately he haven't got much room left on ice and he got no more hope of life. Never sleep much, he been having some meat from that oogruk. One evening he saw some thing it look black—look like getting bigger and bigger every time when he sees it. And he notice it coming toward him.

56

*Every day that ice cake
getting smaller,
melting off.*

It did not take long, that thing he sees come right up to him where he was floating on ice. That thing was floating, too, it look like wood and look square. From that thing that floated and looked like wood and was square—a voice said to him, "Gee, you haven't got any more room on that ice you been floating on. You jump on me and I take you back to your home." So young man jump on. But somebody still talking to young man. "I know you since you lost your kayak and floated on that ice. I want you to make copy of me when you get back to Kotzebue and use me for your wolf dance wooden drum. And use eagle tail feather on each corner of that wooden drum. And put down feather on end of each tail feather, and build me big enough so one man can handle me. Make it fancy on front and side of that wooden drum. And hang me up on ceiling in Kazree when they going to use me." After young man get off on beach that thing roll around and let young man look over him. And young man going back to Kotzebue and that float start straight out to Arctic ocean after he let young man get to Kotzebue Village. He did not wait long, he got Kotzebue man—they talk it over and start making that wolf dance wooden drum. So they made first wolf dance wooden drum at Kotzebue. That where that wolf dance start from in beginning.

Ahgupuk

Early days ago we have dance in Kazree. (That meeting house.)

57

25   Eskimo Dances

SAY, FRIEND, there lot of fun in this Eskimo dance if you learn how. It not hard to learn. It easier than American dances. I could make you expert Eskimo dancer in a week. Maybe you don't think so. But I do.

Eskimo dance is just like fox trot: 1-2, 1-2. Men dance different from woman in Eskimo dance, also woman dance different from men. In what they call real dance for all people, men got to use their feet to keep time, and women don't get to use their feet to keep time, woman using their whole body to keep time, in this real dance.

The other dance we had is motion dance. You got to learn them motion dances first before you dance. You know, we say "Here is bow and arrow dance." We put action how we shoot bow and arrow in that dance.

Every year at Kotzebue we make new Eskimo song and put new motion dance on them. We make up those Eskimo song, we never write it down, we just remember them in our mind.

I move to Kotzebue from Kivalina in 1938. I was the Foreman for CCC at Kivalina in 1937 and transfer 1938 to Kotzebue to be with principal Foreman at Kotzebue. When I arrived to Kotzebue they hardly have any dances, so I talk with my cousins, Abraham Lincoln and Walter Lincoln (two brothers), and Lester Gallahorn. We made plan that we should have dance every Friday night at school house, one Friday night Eskimo dance, next Friday night America dance. I went over to school house and ask teachers what they think about it. They say okey with them. So we start having dances every Friday night at Kotzebue school house, and we bring life to Kotzebue, young people and old people. No matter if old or young, they hardly wait for coming Friday!

58

There lot of fun in this Eskimo dance,
if you learn how.

One Friday we having Eskimo dance, next Friday we having America dance. So one Friday night way before Christmas we having Eskimo dance. One of the white lady came over to me and ask me if I would teach them Eskimo dances. She told me there were five of them CAA and Weather Bureau ladies. I told her "As long as you ladies want to become Eskimo dancer I'll make expert Eskimo dancer out of you!" I told her, "I am going to have you ladies on my program for New Year's Eve." (It was about two weeks before Christmas.) I did not wait for anything. Next day after work, after I eat my supper, I went down to CAA. Because I did not have much time before New Year I start my Eskimo dancing group that night in CAA building. I went down to CAA every night, give them ladies lesson. I had one of the ACS boy to teach Eskimo motion dances beside them ladies.

I wrote down on paper every motion dance I taught to them ladies, and they pick it up quick.

When you learning Eskimo dances, first one is the hardest. Rest of them easier than first.

My cousin, Walter Lincoln, teach three Kotzebue Eskimo girl. My cousin have these three girl every year on New Year's Eve program. So when New Year Eve came, my cousin Walter ask me who going to have his program first.

I said to Walter "You better have your program first."

So Walter have his three young lady motion dancers.

They had three different motion dance, and everybody happy to see them three young ladies doing Eskimo motion dances; and they got through them fine.

For making these Eskimo dance, we have six drummer: Abraham Lincoln, Eli Richard, Walter Lincoln, Earl Wilson, Charley Allen and myself.

I stood up and tell the people (there were lot of people in the school house) I told them in English and in Eskimo language "This is first year we going to see white ladies doing Eskimo motion dance."

Look to me like everybody was surprise; because they don't know any white lady before, doing Eskimo dance, and they don't know I been teaching these five white lady.

Gee, they sure put up good Eskimo dance! Everybody holler "More, more!" They dance six different motion dances. Gee, everybody sure happy about it!

So I could make you good Eskimo dancer any time, if you just wanted to learn. There is a good lot of exercise in Eskimo dance.

That ACS boy (white boy) I taught while I was at Kotzebue, he's become *good* Eskimo dancer. Every time I do motion dance while I was at Kotzebue, he's right there with me. He's getting *very* good. He's out in States now; I never heard from him for long time.

Kobuk people dance little different than we do in Kotzebue; and their song little different from our song, too.

Some of our Eskimo dance is slow motion, like slow waltz; and some of them just like fox trot; and some of them like jitterbug. And some of the song we still remember and sing was made before first white man came to this country of America!

26 How Caribou Hunter Got Lost

EARLY DAYS AGO at Barrow, sometimes caribou hunter got lost, never returned to Barrow. One of the young men at Barrow was just wondering what was become of those hunter. So one summer he start inland

60

Ahgupuk

Dwarf say, "Take your choice first, which way you go." Young man say "Okay, I go this way." So they start apart.

to hunt for caribou. Young man went up inland and he got close to the mountain. You will never see no mountain at Point Lay or Wainwright or Barrow. No mountain around. Mountain way back, can't see it from those village.

Finely, he get to big lake. He walk right along the lake. While he was walking he saw a little man coming toward him. It was dwarf, young man never saw a small man like him before. When they meet, dwarf said to young man, "Let's have foot race around the big lagoon."

And the young man said, "Okay."

Dwarf said to young man, "Take your choice first, which way you want to go. I'll go other way and we'll see who will get around this lake first."

So they start apart. They going around big lagoon and coming to their starting line. Young man came in first. He won foot race.

When dwarf came in he look mad. So dwarf pull out from his side some kind weapon and aim to young man. Young man watch it pretty close. When dwarf throw his weapon at young man, young man jump. Dwarf miss the young man and young man ran after dwarf weapon.

Dwarf ran after it at the same time. But young man caught the dwarfs weapon. When young man caught the dwarfs weapon he turn around and aim at dwarf. So young man act like he throw weapon at dwarf—he fool dwarf, and dwarf jump up in air. While dwarf was in the air, young man throw that weapon and caught dwarf right in the middle of his body.

When dwarf come down, dwarf got no more fight left. Young man understand dwarf when he talk—dwarf told young man he had a wife and three kids. Dwarf told young man where his family was and told him to go and tell his family to go back to rest of their folk.

But dwarf told young man, "Be sure to sneak up on my family, otherwise you won't find them." Dwarf said, "You tell my wife that you kill me to protect yourself. I had two boys growing, and tell them I sent my last words to them. Tell them don't act like I am. My wife told me lot of time not to go after man's life. She said, I'll be kill some day if I'm doing that. But I thought there is nobody could get best of me. But I know now. But it too late. Don't be afraid to tell my wife that you kill me to protect yourself. Just tell her to go back to rest of her folk."

Dwarf told young man, "I been kill lot of man like you when they were hunting around here. But now no more. I talk enough now, so you can finish me now. But the last thing I ask you: bury my body but take my head off and lay it on top of flat rock. No game will bother it, but lot of hunter will see my skull."

And young man finish dwarf and cut his head off and buried his body and put his head on top of flat rock.

Few man from Kivalina been seen dwarf skull on top of flat rock way back from Point Barrow close to mountain. Anakok Sage been seen that skull, and Earl Wilson, and Father Potkak, and more men beside them, too. They say dwarf skull is about size swan egg.

And now about his wife. After young man buried dwarf body and put his skull on top flat rock, he start to find dwarf family. When he seem to get close, he watch pretty close. Finely, young man saw them first before they see him. He went right up to them before they see him. When he get right close to them, he showed himself up. Those two boy disappear, but their mother stay—don't move.

Young man walk up to dwarf wife and told her about everything what her husband want him to tell her. And young man told dwarf wife that he buried her husband body. And young man told lady that her husband sent his last word to his two sons. And the lady called her two sons and they came over.

Their mother told the boys, "Your father sent word by this man to tell us. You boys listen to him, he will tell you boys what your father said."

And the young man told the boys what happen, how they meet first place—having foot race and their father tried to kill him first and he was killed by young man. "And your father said," the young man said to boys, "he was told by you boy's mother that he should not go after a man's life, in case some day he will be killed. So he said he don't think

When young man found dwarf wife she had three kids. One girl and two boys. She carry girl on her back.

there will be anybody will get best of him. But there was somebody. Now he said in his last word, 'be sure you go up and tell my wife and my two boys what happen to me. Tell my boys I said, Don't bother anybody as long as they leave you alone. Tell my family to go back to their folks.' That what you boy daddy told me to come and tell you folk. What all happen between you boys daddy and me."

So dwarf wife said, "I told my husband lot of time not to bother any hunter. But my husband never listen to what I said to him. Now he's dead. I take my family back to the rest of our folks."

When young man found dwarf wife she had three kids. One girl and two boys. She carry girl on her back. Those two boys sure can move around.

And that weapon that dwarf got was ivory, sharp up.

Lot of Eskimo think there are dwarfs living Alaska some place, because sometimes they saw their footprints on mud up the river.

Ahgupuk

Our old generation used to tell us kids. They tell us how to do things, and in evening they tell us stories of early days ago.

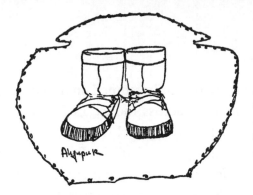

If we clean our mukluk with fresh snow and take salt out, mukluk freeze and break up on us.

Drifted in Arctic Ocean   27

THERE WAS A MAN named Sa-ma-roo-na live twelve mile above Kivalina with his family up the coast. So he was drifted on ice two or three times in his life in the Arctic Ocean. But he made his home every time when he was drifted. He never have kayak, he just got his gun and hunting gear with him.

When he telling us sometime about drifting he was saying, every time when he find out that he was drifted out he always started to go way out —straight out—till he find old heavy ice that got old snow and he made snow igloo and stay there till the storm is over. When the storm is over he start toward land, always find land and come home safe.

But he said first time when he drifted he made one big mistake when he landed on land. He told us how first time when he drift out when he land he went up to main land right away and clean his mukluk on fresh snow. He said after he clean it off he started home on main land, he knew family camp not very far from where he land.

He said he didn't go very far when his mukluk freeze up on him and break up the bottom of his mukluk. So he said he tore piece from his storm calico parkie and wrap his feet. He said he was lucky that he landed close to family camped on the coast. Sa-ma-roo-na say if any man couldn't make it across the ice in first place when he started to drift out, don't try to stay right close to open lead—start right out straight to get away from open lead till he find old ice with old snow on it and make snow igloo, and stay there till storm is over if he want to get home safe.

Sa-ma-roo-na is pretty nice old man, he don't want to keep what he learn for hisself, he want young generation to know what to do, if they happen to be drifted out in Arctic Ocean.

In the year of 1939 on the month of March, there were bunch of us went out seal hunting from Kotzebue and some hunter from Kobuk. Before we get to open water we make camp. It was getting late.

Next morning we start out early and we get to open water. There were Eli Richard and Richard Scott and myself, we go along together on the open lead going toward South. I caught one seal all that day— about noon. Wind coming up. We looking for good place to camp so we found old ice and we made a camp there.

We dig in hard snow about four feet down and use canvas for top. We made nice home sweet home big enough for three of us, and we cooked fresh seal meat for supper and tea. Gee, all of us enjoy our fresh seal meat for supper.

In that first night big storm came up. When we wake next morning when we went out we couldn't see anything, getting cloudy all over and we could see black cloud on back of us toward land. Gee, talk about snow blowing!

We talk to each other when we went in to our home sweet home that we been drifted out. And we talk to each other we can't do anything, it so stormy like this and we said we got to wait till the storm is over, and I told them other two boys what Sa-ma-roo-na use to tell us while I

66

was at Kivalina, because these two boy with me were from Kotzebue, they don't know what Sa-ma-roo-na been telling Kivalina boy.

So we was storm bound for three-four day. Fourth day in the morning we wake up early—we never hear storm. So we get up make coffee, make breakfast. After breakfast I went out. When I went out, gee, it sure was good weather, no wind, clear. So we broke our camp down, loaded our sled and started home.

We could hardly see any mountains when we first start. We just see one little peak of the highest mountain across from Kotzebue. So it took us three days to get home to Kotzebue from where we drifted. We was lucky!

It a rough life to be on the other side of open water. Every seal hunter should watch when they hunt for seal in winter time. On that last night when we camp on thin ice we got nothing to make hot coffee or tea. Everything salty—no old snow on thin ice.

After we put up tent I walk way out from tent about 50 feet, here I saw old snow on top of ice just like somebody put it there. I call my two partners to come over and see what I found before I touch it. So we get canvas and put that old snow in it and take it over to our tent.

Sea ice becomes fresh after one season. In the spring the ice is already fresh on top.

On the ice we use old snow for fresh water, make coffee or tea.

67

*In those days herder never use dog team.
They use reindeer like driving horse with wagon.*

Ahgupuk

28 How to Train Reindeer Herd

FIRST TIME I seen reindeer, I was just a little husky kid. They had government herd, with them reindeer all in one herd when they started. So later, I don't know how many years later, they divided them herd in two. They have Elooktoona for chief herder for one herd—and they have Ootpalee chief herder for other herd. Elooktoona herd were in North Kivalina River, and Ootpalee herd in Kivalina South River. They were having native boy from Kivalina and Point Hope help Elooktoona and Ootpalee herd government herd.

Around 1924 there were five different herd around Kivalina. And around 1928 I became herder and went work for Chester Seveck. Chester Seveck he's chief herder today for government herd at Kotzebue.

There were hardly any wolf those days. When I were herder we took care of our herds. Those day in the spring fawning time, we watch our herd day and nights. We never let our herd go stray.

Later, Kivalina and Noatak form company, and after they form company they let herd go stray in summer and rounded up early in fall after freeze-up. They tried to keep expense down.

In summer they keep small herd up for butcher for meat, and they ship meat out on Boxer*. Later they ship meat out on North Star*.

*Boxer and North Star were ships operated by the Alaska Native Service.

68

In the last count we chute reindeer through corral. We count 45,000 head owned by Kivalina and Noatak Company. That were last time we seen Kivalina and Noatak Company herd—the Kivalina and Noatak Company herd disappear—eaten by wolf. I think if they keep those reindeer like they keep it early days ago they would have some reindeer left today.

When I became reindeer herder, first thing our chief herder taught me how to broke in sled deer. It is lot of fun to break sled deer. In those day, herder never use dog team, they use reindeer team like driving horse with wagon—but they never have saddle on reindeer like cowboy does to horse, like Roy Rogers and Gene Autry.

Here how you break sled deer: Take about six feet rope. First thing, tie deer to clump of grass. Let deer been tie to clump of grass all night. Next morning untie deer and put long line on and start to work it from front. Pull the deer ahead from front and pretty soon deer will follow you by line. Deer won't let line get tight after he learn how to follow.

After you get deer learn how to follow, you then put harness on deer and put long tow-line to sled and start your deer. After you get your deer started—jump in sled and have good ride!

After deer learn to follow, put harness on deer and put long tow line to sled and start your deer.

After you use your sled deer for three or four day, make your tow-line shorter. Every time you put harness on deer be careful you don't let deer jump around. If you careful with deer for few days your deer will get used to it and pretty soon will never jump around when you start to put harness on it. Pretty soon you will have short tow-line—about six feet tow-line—on your harness.

It lot of fun to drive sled deer. While I was at Kivalina I used to go trapping with boy in inland with sled deer. We started from Kivalina when fox season open and came home when fox season close.

Sled deer go long way when you took good care of them. In those early days Elooktoona and Ootpalee carried U.S. mail up to Point Barrow by reindeer team all through winter. Sometimes they have to stop day or two for blizzard—but mail always get through.

29 Eskimo Duck Hunt and Fight

ONCE UPON A TIME one spring at Point Hope when eider duck came through, Ah-lu-ruk and his three brother went to Point for hunting duck with sling shot. They used to tie seven sling shot together and use them for ducks.

You know my friend, this is how they make them sling shot for duck. They took seven piece of any kind of bones or seven piece of ivory and rounded them up like chicken eggs shape and tie about twenty-four inches string on each one of them.

End of those string they tie together to duck feather; so as to hold the duck sling. When you throw them sling them ivory egg spread out and when they hit a duck they tangle on a duck and duck drop down like you shot with shot gun.

70

They used to tie seven sling shot together and use for duck sling.

Ahgupuk

Ah-lu-ruk and his brothers went to Point for hunting duck with sling.

In that same day Kee-na-vee-ruk's uncle and his partner went to Point for duck hunting with sling (I forgot Kee-na-vee-ruk's uncle name). Kee-na-vee-ruk's uncle and his partner they hunt together all time. (Some time they change with their wife for two-three days and have their wife back again.) And them two partner was next to Ah-lu-ruk's brothers, they were waiting for duck flying.

Soon they saw big flock of duck coming. That big flock of duck come right through between Ah-lu-ruk and them two partner. (In those early day them Eskimo had rule any time when duck fell without any sling on it first man that pick it up always have it.) Finally Ah-lu-ruk brothers and them two partner throw their sling; none of them get any, they only saw one duck fell without any sling on him.

They ran after that duck. Kee-na-vee-ruk's uncle pick it up first and bring the duck to his partner. (They have blind made out of snow, there were lot of snow yet that time.) He put duck in side of their blind. While they getting their sling ready here Ah-lu-ruk coming over.

When Ah-lu-ruk get to them two partner, he pick the duck up without word and take it over to his brothers. After Ah-lu-ruk left with duck, that other partner saying to Kee-na-vee-ruk's uncle "What did Ah-lu-ruk think we are, kids or something? Maybe Ah-lu-ruk think we worst than a dog!"

Finally Kee-na-vee-ruk's uncle said, "Maybe Ah-lu-ruk think that what we are," and Kee-na-vee-ruk's uncle stood up and went over to Ah-lu-ruk's brothers. When he get to them he pick up the duck without a word and bring it back to his partner. When he get to his partner he lay the duck again inside their blind. (They were some distance apart, them duck hunter Ah-lu-ruk's brothers and Kee-na-vee-ruk's uncle and his partner.)

Here Ah-lu-ruk jump out from his brothers with bow and arrow. That Kee-na-vee-ruk's uncle didn't have his bow and arrow with him. Kee-na-vee-ruk's uncle said to his partner, "I did not have my bow and arrow with me, I left it home." His partner said, "Why don't you use my bow and arrow? It same as yours." So Kee-na-vee-ruk's uncle try his partner bow and arrow—they were too strong for him.

His partner told him to cut some sinew on back of that bow and arrow. So Kee-na-vee-ruk uncle cut some of the sinew string on back of his partner bow and arrow. Made it just right for him and he went down to meet Ah-lu-ruk with bow and arrow.

Ah-lu-ruk want Kee-na-vee-ruk's uncle to start the fight. But Kee-na-vee-ruk's uncle told Ah-lu-ruk, "You the man started the fight—why don't you finish it?" So Ah-lu-ruk shot Kee-na-vee-ruk's uncle with bow and arrow, but miss. They been shooting at each other for while but they miss each other.

We make duck blind of snow blocks when we go hunting duck.

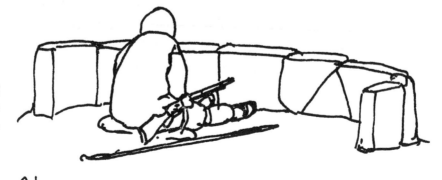

Ahgupuk

Finally Kee-na-vee-ruk's uncle wounded Ah-lu-ruk, got him on his upper leg, so Ah-lu-ruk could not stand any more. So Kee-na-vee-ruk's uncle went up to his partner, never do anything more to Ah-lu-ruk, and went home with his partner. They never told anybody at their village about their fight with Ah-lu-ruk with bow and arrow. Next day Kee-na-vee-ruk's uncle and his partner hear the news that Ah-lu-ruk hurt his leg at Point by falling on rough ice.

Every morning Kee-na-vee-ruk's uncle and his partner when they start out hunt they went by Ah-lu-ruk igloo and call in through sky light—and saying to Ah-lu-ruk they were going out hunt. They sure make Ah-lu-ruk mad! But Ah-lu-ruk cannot help it, he was badly wounded. All spring when them two partner went out hunting they come by Ah-lu-ruk igloo and stop and call in through sky light, they were going out hunting. Finally summer came. Them two partners never get apart, they stayed together all time. And Ah-lu-ruk got well and winter came and ocean froze. They start hunting seal, oogruk, and bear.

One day Kee-na-vee-ruk's uncle went out hunt alone. That the last time when Kee-na-vee-ruk saw his uncle, in the morning when he left for hunting seal and bear. Kee-na-vee-ruk's uncle partner and Kee-na-vee-ruk was wondering what become of his uncle. Nobody know. Kee-na-vee-ruk become a man, when his uncle disappear. Kee-na-vee-ruk was raise by his uncle. Kee-na-vee-ruk's both parent died and when they died his uncle took Kee-na-vee-ruk and raise him up.

One day at noon Kee-na-vee-ruk was standing outdoor on side of his igloo. Here he saw one of Ah-lu-ruk's youngest brother coming toward him. Kee-na-vee-ruk was waiting for him. When Ah-lu-ruk's brother get to Kee-na-vee-ruk he said that their own brother Ah-lu-ruk mad at them. Ah-lu-ruk's brother said to Kee-na-vee-ruk, "We three brother hoping to have our own brother kill by somebody, because he don't do any good for us. You know early this winter your uncle never come home from his seal hunting?"

Kee-na-vee-ruk say, "Yes."

"Our brother Ah-lu-ruk kill your uncle. This is the way it start. Our brother Ah-lu-ruk make us stop between two ice berg where no one could see us from distance. While we were there your uncle came. When your uncle sees us he stop. As soon he stop our brother Ah-lu-ruk stood up and walk over to your uncle, and said to your uncle, 'Let us have wrestle.'

"Your uncle took off his hunting gear and they start wrestle. Your uncle throw our brother down. After he throw him down he start to stand up, but our brother keep holding on him—they keep wrestling for while. Your uncle throw our brother every time. We three brother just watch them two wrestle.

"Then our brother throw your uncle down, when he throw him down he won't let your uncle stand up, he hold him down and he call us to come over and help him. So we went over to help our brother.

"He told us to pull your uncle mitten off so we did. When he pull his mitten off he was on his bare hand. He try to stand up and have his bare hand on slush salty thin ice. His bare hand getting white, freezing up. When his hand freeze, our brother Ah-lu-ruk let him go, and ran over to our hunting gear, grab his bow and arrow and start shooting your uncle.

"Our brother miss your uncle, and your uncle try to shoot our brother. But the string of his bow cut the skin off his hand that been froze and he can't do anything with bow and arrow. Our brother kill your uncle then.

Your uncle took off his hunting gear and they start wrestle.

"After our brother kill your uncle we cut hole in the ice and shove your uncle under the ice. So you know now how your uncle been kill by our brother Ah-lu-ruk. If you kill our brother Ah-lu-ruk we won't mind. We will just treat you like our own brother after you kill our brother Ah-lu-ruk."

So Kee-na-vee-ruk thank Ah-lu-ruk brother that he now know what happen to his uncle.

Summer came through and fall time ground freezing up. They have two big meeting igloo, what they call Ka-zree in Eskimo. They have name for both meeting igloo. Upper Ka-zree they call Ka-ma-toak Ka-zree, lower Ka-zree they call Oo-gu-see-see-guk.

So Kee-na-vee-ruk belong to Ka-ma-toak Ka-zree and Ah-lu-ruk brother belong to Oo-gu-see-see-guk Ka-zree. Every fall in those days they having games of foot ball between them two Ka-zree. Once a while old man come in to Ka-zree where Kee-na-vee-ruk was. Kee-na-vee-ruk was making bow and arrow. This old man was saying that Ah-lu-ruk been going after our Ka-zree people and push them hard try to make them scared.

So Kee-na-vee-ruk stood up and say, "I wonder who will fix my bow and arrow? I hear that Ah-lu-ruk been kill my uncle."

People at Point Hope never seen Kee-na-vee-ruk play any kind of game. Never come around where they having games; so one old man told Kee-na-vee-ruk, "Hand it to me. I fix it for you."

So Kee-na-vee-ruk went out from Ka-zree and went down to the game of foot ball. He tried to get close to the ball and watch the people same time. Here he see Ah-lu-ruk every time when he get close to anybody that go after ball, he try to shove them hard and try to scare them.

So Kee-na-vee-ruk getting closer to the ball. Kee-na-vee-ruk's partner kick the ball toward Kee-na-vee-ruk. When Kee-na-vee-ruk go after the ball, here come Ah-lu-ruk. When Ah-lu-ruk get close to Kee-na-vee-ruk Ah-lu-ruk push Kee-na-vee-ruk hard, but Kee-na-vee-ruk hold himself up with his arm. He did not fall to the ground when he get pushed.

Kee-na-vee-ruk get to the ball first then and kick the ball with his foot, and run after the ball again so here he see Ah-lu-ruk running to that ball same time he does. Kee-na-vee-ruk let Ah-lu-ruk pass him. When Ah-lu-ruk get close to the ball Kee-na-vee-ruk run after Ah-lu-ruk from behind and push him hard. Then he just pay no attention to Ah-lu-ruk but keep going after the ball.

While Kee-na-vee-ruk was running somebody grab him behind. When Kee-na-vee-ruk look, it was Ah-lu-ruk. Ah-lu-ruk try to put his arm around Kee-na-vee-ruk—want to wrestle. Kee-na-vee-ruk told Ah-lu-ruk they never do like that in ball game. But Ah-lu-ruk won't stop. He want to wrestle with Kee-na-vee-ruk. So they wrestle.

Every time Kee-na-vee-ruk throw Ah-lu-ruk down, but Ah-lu-ruk hang on to Kee-na-vee-ruk every time when Kee-na-vee-ruk stand up. Finally Kee-na-vee-ruk look around to see if any hump on the ground while he have his arm around Ah-lu-ruk. He saw hump and Kee-na-vee-ruk throw Ah-lu-ruk right on that hump and Kee-na-vee-ruk landed on top of Ah-lu-ruk hard.

Kee-na-vee-ruk hear Ah-lu-ruk grunt, and when Kee-na-vee-ruk stood up Ah-lu-ruk did not hang on to him. Ah-lu-ruk was still laying on top of that hump and Ah-lu-ruk bleeding through his mouth. And Kee-na-vee-ruk get hold Ah-lu-ruk on arm and tell him to stand up so they can wrestle some more.

But Ah-lu-ruk say, "No!"

76

And Kee-na-vee-ruk say, "Get up quick!" He pull Ah-lu-ruk by his arm and say to him, "Let us have more wrestle. I heard you let my uncle try to stand up with his bare hand on slush salty thin ice. Get up now, you fool, after you kill my uncle you try to have me put pity on you?"

And Ah-lu-ruk said to Kee-na-vee-ruk, "That enough, you done me enough."

So Ah-lu-ruk last till midnight and then he died. And those three brothers of Ah-lu-ruk treated Kee-na-vee-ruk just like their own brother. Stayed with him some time, go hunting with him, and do everything for him.

Seal, Oogruk and Walrus— 30
What They Made of by Eskimo

IN ARCTIC OF ALASKA, we call big bearded seal oogruk. They big seal, bigger than hair seal, but not so big as walrus. Oogruk (bearded seal) is not compare to walrus. Walrus is big animal two or three time as big as oogruk. But they both were good eating. Na-koo. (Na-koo mean good.) And the hair scal is smaller than spotted seal.

We Eskimo use all them seal, oogruk, walrus for lot of things. You don't waste anything out of them animals if you know how to take care of them. Mama Eskimo make good dried meat out of oogruk meat. Out of blubber she made good oil like Wesson oil.

Now about oogruk gut. Mama Eskimo clean oogruk gut. After she clean it she wash it in water. After it dried it ready to use for skylight. Eskimo mama do the same thing to walrus guts. You can have your rain parkie

77

Walrus is big animal, two or three times as big as oogruk. Good eating.

made out of oogruk or walrus guts, and we use walrus stomach for our Eskimo drum skin. Eskimo drum is the music to use in Eskimo dance to keep time.

Early days ago Eskimo use oogruk guts and walrus guts for sail for boat also for small tent. You know oogruk guts and walrus guts is waterproof and windproof. Walrus skin they use it to cover their skin boat. (Oomiak) Seal skin and oogruk skin they use for make rope. Oogruk skin they use it to make the bottom of their mukluk. (mukluk Eskimo shoes).

When Papa Eskimo get seal or oogruk, his wife cut the hide different for rope than for mukluk. For rope, Mama Eskimo put seal skin or oogruk skin in blubber and keep in oil until hair come out from hide. When hair come out from hide, Mama Eskimo clean the skin. After she clean the skin, Papa Eskimo sharp up his knife, and make rope out of oogruk skin or seal skin. He cut skin around and round in one long strip. That how Papa Eskimo make his rope.

He uses seal rope for making sled and snowshoe; they used it for harpoon line, also for tow-line. Seal rope come handy for everything.

Oogruk rope is pretty strong rope. We also make rope out of young walrus; they make good rope.

Mama Eskimo make white skin out of seal skin, in wintertime. You know, Mama Eskimo put raw seal skin in blubber and keep in blubber until hair come out. When hair come out, she took it out from oil and scrape it with her knife. Then she put it in water and soak it and change water every day and put soap in water.

When oil all come out of skin, she clean the skin inside the house. After she clean it, she took it out and stretch it in cold weather and freeze it and keep it out door till dry. The skin become white skin when dry and then Mama Eskimo use it for mukluk top. That make waterproof mukluk.

78

*Papa Eskimo sharpen up his knife
to cut oogruk skin or seal skin.*

Sometimes they dried up the seal skin with hair on and use for mukluk tops.

You can make lot of thing out of hair seal skin. You can make mukluk, rope, pants, mitten, parkie. Same way with spotted seal skin. Spotted seal skin little heavier—better to use for parkie, wear better. Hair seal use for pants, little softer—bend more easy.

How Mama Eskimo Make Ice Cream   31

MAMA ESKIMO use reindeer or caribou fat for making ice cream. She took fat and chop it up fine. After chop it up, rounded it up again put it in a pan, and heat it a little. After she heat little she put seal oil and water on fine snow and start to work with hand and stir it up.

Pretty soon that fat getting white and getting bigger and bigger. Pretty soon she have pan full of Eskimo ice cream. When she have pan full of ice cream, she add berries, any kind berries you want. Some time she use meat instead of berries, chopped up some meat and added to ice cream.

Now today sometimes they use raisin or dried apple. They cook dried apple and raisin then add Eskimo ice cream. Gee, it sure good. Na-koo! (that mean fine) They use seal oil or water more than once, depend on ice cream how it look. Some time they use fish, cook fish, boiled. After fish boiled they took all the bone out and squeeze the fish, take all the juice out and use it for ice cream.

It did not take much of reindeer or caribou fat to make pan full of Eskimo ice cream. Let me tell you something my friend, that why Eskimo in the Arctic of Alaska never waste reindeer or caribou fat. They use everything they can when they get any kind of wild games.

Wesson oil is about same as seal oil.

79

They cut skin round and round in one long strip.
That how they make rope.

*There are woods along the Noatak River
and those Noatak people have log cabin.
From here north to Barrow,
only a little brush sometimes.*

32 Noatak—Alaska

THOSE PEOPLE of Noatak in spring time, some of them went down the coast for seal hunting. They went overland down the coast with dog team and with their skin boats and their family. They leave Noatak Village on last part of April and they spend little over month on the coast and went to Shesualik and hunt for white whale—Beluga, and them other Noatak people that was left at Noatak village, they move away from their village to their muskrat camp and hunt for muskrat while muskrat season open.

After muskrat season close they went down the river with boats after ice goes out and get down to Shesualik and meet other Noatak people that went down the coast for seal hunt. And all the Noatak people get together again at Shesualik and stay at Shesualik part of June and July hunting together for white whale, Beluga. And they get lot of Beluga meat and muktuk. They dry Beluga meat and cook Beluga muktuk and put them muktuk in barrel or seal poke with oil and save them for winter.

And around August them Noatak people went across to Kotzebue Village and stay for a month in Kotzebue Village and in September them Noatak people they all left for their home up the river at Noatak village for winter. And when they get home to Noatak village in September they start fishing—dry up fish. There are woods along Noatak river. They cut wood and make raft—then they raft wood to their village for winter. They had salmon trout and white fish and some other fish.

It look to me them Noatak people do more travel around than rest of the villages.

How Ka-ya-yeah-tow-look Get His Woman 33

ONE UPON A TIME Ka-ya-yeah-tow-look and his sister live at Kivalina. South river, way up the river about forty mile from beach. They were all by them self. Their parents been dead quite while back. There were more Kivalina people below them on same river, also North river. Kivalina had two rivers. South river they call it in Eskimo, Oo-lik. North river Ke-va-lik.

So one day Ka-ya-yeah-tow-look think his sister should have some one else to talk to. So young man Ka-ya-yeah-tow-look left toward Noatak Village. So next day he get close to Noatak village.

He look around and watch everything, finally he saw bunch of woman picking berries. He sneak up to them and watch them, he saw one of the lady was good looking lady. He was hoping that lady should be alone. Finally that lady become all by herself, other woman was quite away from her. So Ka-ya-yeah-tow-look jump and put something around her mouth so the rest of the woman don't hear her.

Ka-ya-yeah-tow-look took the lady home to his sister. And those woman when they went home to Noatak village they told their folk one of the lady disappear while they picking berries. They said they were looking for her but they not find her, nowhere.

The snow come and freeze up. So Ka-ya-yeah-tow-look fix up his sled and they started to Noatak. His wife and his sister. They only got two or three dog (early day ago they don't have many dogs like to-day). Ka-ya-yeah-tow-look told his wife they will stop with her parents.

They arrived to Noatak Village when it get dark. Nobody know who they are, till the lady went to her parents igloo, then they find out.

Everybody was happy when they find out that lady disappear last fall come home with nice young man and nice young lady. Ka-ya-yeah-tow-look sister got nice husband from Noatak village in that first trip they made to Noatak, and they all four went back to Kivalina river where Ka-ya-yeah-tow-look and his sister's home was.

Ka-ya-yeah-tow-look took that
Noatak young lady home to his sister.

Ahgupuk

ONCE UPON A TIME there was a young man name Ah-seo-na-yat; he was
in a village with the rest of the people. When they having Eskimo
dance he was right there with them and dance.

Sometime when they were dancing Ah-seo-na-yat told rest of the people, in his village, even if he die he will do the dancing. So one summer
Ah-seo-na-yat got sick and he died. When Ah-seo-na-yat died they were
burying him in little mound by the river. Once in a while they were having dance but Ah-seo-na-yat never showed up in dance.

One time in summer there were three oomiak (that skin boat) that went
by Ah-seo-na-yat grave. Two of the oomiak get way ahead. They left one
oomiak way behind. It was just wife and husband in that oomiak they left
behind. Them two oomiak that get way ahead they had lot of people in
their oomiak. So them two oomiak get under Ah-seo-na-yat grave and so
one of the person from one of them two oomiak holler to Ah-seo-na-yat
grave. "Where, where Ah-seo-na-yat? He always say even if he died he
was going to dance."

Them two, wife and husband, in oomiak that got left way behind, they
heard the voice from somebody that holler to Ah-seo-na-yat grave from
one of them boat. Then Ah-seo-na-yat coming up from his grave using
shoulder blade for drum and using one of forearm bone for drumstick.
So Ah-seo-na-yat was hopping, jumping and dancing around his grave.

When he finish his song he holler, "Oooy—ooy," and them two oomiak
turn over every time when Ah-seo-na-yat went back to his grave. Not
even one person in them two oomiak was save. Every one of them drown.
So when wife and husband that got left way behind, when they get to
their village they told their people what happen to them other two oomiak.

83

*Ah-seo-na-yat coming up from grave
and dancing around his grave.*

They told their people that Ah-seo-na-yat was telling the truth when he say even when he died he will do the dance.

And they say, "But don't bother Ah-seo-na-yat in his grave anymore, that why them people lost their lives, tried to make fun out of Ah-seo-na-yat. Let Ah-seo-na-yat rest in peace and don't bother him any more."

35 Games and Blanket Toss

EARLY DAYS AGO they used to have lot of games. Eskimo now today, they hardly have games. Early days ago nearly every evening in winter time they having football game. Old men, young men and woman too, when the weather is good. In summer when they don't have anything to do they having football games and other games. They having kicking contest with both feet—trying to touch rope. Also they having rope tricks, like pulling self up with one arm—and all sorts of tricks.

Around Kotzebue during Christmas week till New Year they used to have lot of game. All kind of games. Men dog race, and woman dog race,

They have both feet kicking contest, trying to touch rope.

Ahgupuk

Also they have rope tricks,
like pulling self up with one arm.

Ahgupuk

also snowshoe race. They having these races outdoors day time. At evening they started another games inside house, both feet kicking contest, rabbit jump kicking contest, one leg kicking contest.

One time a fellow name Walter Lincoln he raise kicking contest up to ten feet, nine inches with both feet! Nobody get that record yet at Kotzebue. Lot of Eskimo games was fun to watch it.

85

Say, folks, it lot of fun to be in blanket toss. We use walrus skin for blanket toss. Men or woman get around the skin and get hold of the skin and have somebody in the middle of skin. They throw the person up and down. Sometime they throw a person, lady or man, way up in the air and have him or she landed back in the middle of the skin. It is lot of fun to watch it. I been in blanket toss lot of time when I was young age. After my brother caught whale at Point Hope he put up feast and dance and then we have blanket toss.

Say, friend, you might try that blanket toss.

If you do, get in the middle of the skin, and stand on your feet. Please don't watch down, watch on the horizon way off. These people that hold the skin they watch you after they throw you up in the air. They will have you landed in the middle of the skin. Here the other thing you should know. When you get in blanket toss, don't try to jump. Let them people throw you up in the air. Suppose you watch down when they throw you up, it look way down even when they didn't throw you high. Try some time, friend, when you come to Alaska.

END

When you try blanket toss, don't watch down.
They will have you landed in middle of the skin.

About the Author and the Illustrator

A half century ago, writer Abbe Abbott of Anchorage, Alaska, met Paul "Aknik" Green of Kotzebue. Fascinated with Aknik's stories about life in northwestern Alaska, she suggested that he put them on paper. A couple of years later, Abbott was surprised to receive more than fifty handwritten stories from Aknik, with the accompanying note: "I write that book you tell me to write." On paper, his stories were recorded just as if he were talking to the reader one on one—simple, honest, direct, authentic.

With Abbott's assistance, Aknik's stories were first published in serial form in *The Alaska Sportsman* magazine, edited by Robert A. Henning. The editor was so impressed by the collection that in 1959, he decided to publish the stories as a book. I AM ESKIMO would become the first title in Henning's fledgling book-publishing business that is now Alaska Northwest Books®, the premier publisher of books on Alaskan subjects.

Iñupiat artist George Aden Ahgupuk provided the pen-and-ink illustrations of Eskimo life. Ahgupuk once lived in a sod-and-driftwood house on the shores of the Chukchi Sea. Later, he moved his family to Anchorage, several hundred miles to the south. As a youngster, seal hunting with his father, Ahgupuk would draw in the time-honored fashion of the Iñupiat Eskimo, sketching the events of the day and the stories of his elders in pen and ink. After a chance meeting with world-famous artist Rockwell Kent, Ahgupuk's work found national attention and acclaim. Soon Ahgupuk gained an international reputation. In his lengthy career, Ahgupuk's art was displayed in numerous exhibitions and won many prizes, including the Grand Prize of Mexico.

Paul Green, Abbe Abbott, and George Aden Ahgupuk have passed away in the many years since I AM ESKIMO was first published. Their children and grandchildren have granted their approval in bringing this Alaska classic back into print. Our thanks to Paul Green's granddaughter, Mary Viveiros; George Ahgupuk's children, Ralph Ahgupuk, Ruth Floyd, and Robert Lee Ahgupuk; and Abbe Abbott's daughter, Neville Jacobs.

CPSIA information can be obtained
at www.ICGtesting.com
Printed in the USA
BVHW051457020222
627877BV00015B/366